The
MORRIS MINOR
100^

DRIVER'S H

British Leyland (Austin-Morris) Limited
LONGBRIDGE · BIRMINGHAM · ENGLAND

Publication Part No. AKD 3922 (17th Edition)

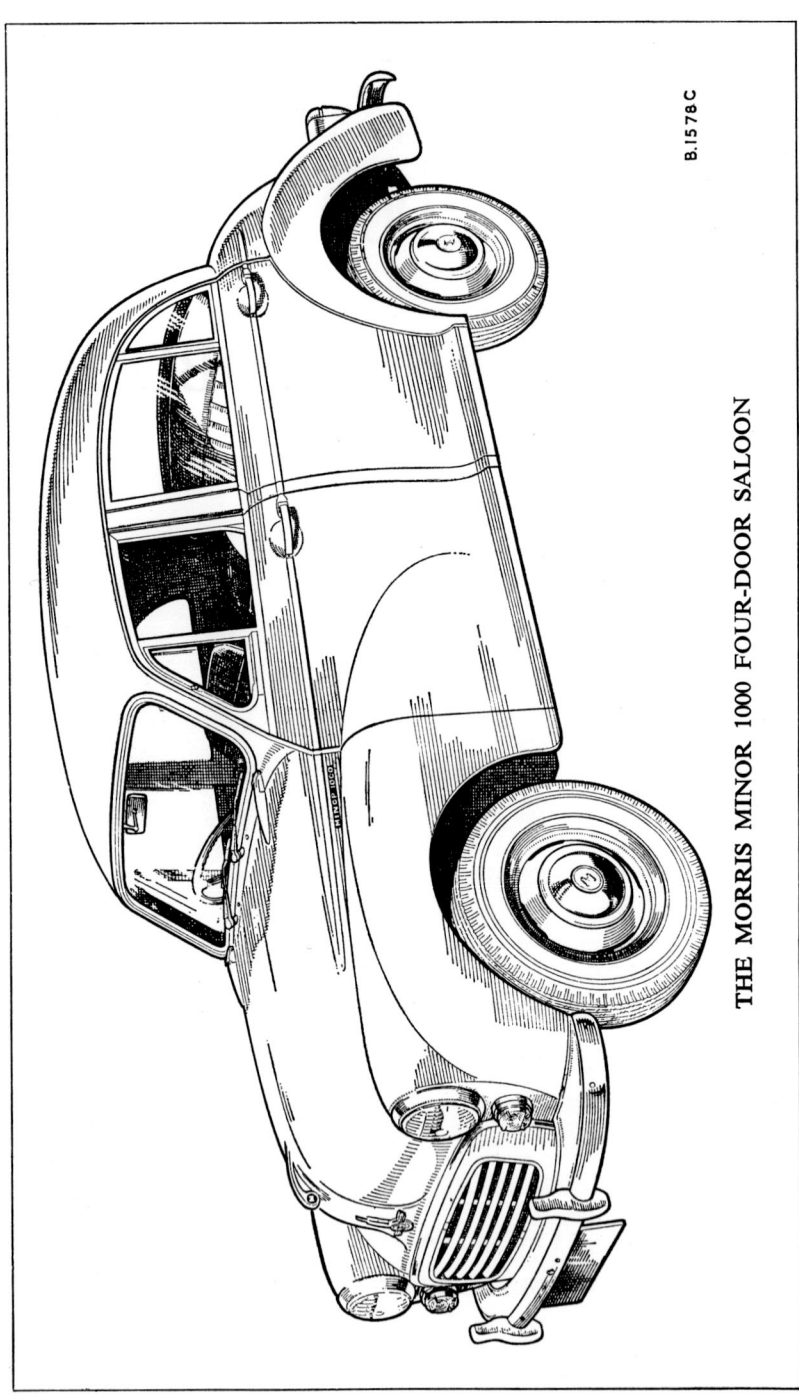

THE MORRIS MINOR 1000 FOUR-DOOR SALOON

B.1578C

FOREWORD

THIS Handbook provides an introduction to your car together with information on the care and periodic maintenance required to combine trouble-free motoring with minimal running costs.

Please note that references to right- or left-hand in this Handbook are made when viewing the car from the rear.

Specification

Specification details set out in this Handbook apply to a range of vehicles and not to any particular vehicle. For the specification of any particular vehicle owners should consult their Distributor or Dealer.

The Manufacturers reserve the right to vary their specifications with or without notice, and at such times and in such manner as they think fit. Major as well as minor changes may be involved in accordance with the Manufacturer's policy of constant product improvement.

Whilst every effort is made to ensure the accuracy of the particulars contained in this Handbook, neither the Manufacturer nor the Distributor or Dealer by whom this Handbook is supplied shall in any circumstances be held liable for any inaccuracy or the consequences thereof.

Maintenance

Your Distributor or Dealer is provided with the latest information concerning special service tools and workshop techniques. This enables him to undertake your service and repairs in the most efficient and economic manner.

Owners are recommended to use the Maintenance Voucher Scheme. A Passport to Service containing service vouchers is provided and regular use of the vouchers in sequence is the best safeguard against the possibility of abnormal repair bills at a later date. Failure to have your car correctly maintained could invalidate the terms of the Warranty.

Completed voucher counterfoils are proof of regular servicing and could well enhance the value of your vehicle in the eyes of a prospective buyer. A replacement Passport to Service voucher book is obtainable from Distributors or Dealers.

Service Parts

Genuine BRITISH LEYLAND and UNIPART Service parts are designed and tested for your vehicle and have the full backing of the British Leyland Factory Warranty. ONLY WHEN GENUINE BRITISH LEYLAND or UNIPART SERVICE PARTS ARE USED CAN RESPONSIBILITY BE CONSIDERED UNDER THE TERMS OF THE WARRANTY.

Genuine parts are supplied in cartons bearing one or both of these symbols.

Service division
COWLEY · OXFORD · ENGLAND

GENERAL DATA

Engine

Type	10MA, 10ME and 10V
Bore	2·543 in. (64·58 mm.)
Stroke	3·296 in. (83·72 mm.)
Cubic capacity	67 cu. in. (1098 c.c.)
Compression ratio: High	8·5 : 1
Low	7·5 : 1
Firing order	1, 3, 4, 2
Valve clearance (cold)	·012 in. (·30 mm.)

Ignition

Sparking plugs	Champion N5, 14 mm.
Sparking plug gap	·025 in. (·64 mm.)
Static timing	3° B.T.D.C.
Stroboscopic timing	6° B.T.D.C. at 600 r.p.m.
Contact breaker gap	·014 to ·016 in. (·36 to ·40 mm.)

Fuel system

Recommended octane rating: H.C. ..	96
L.C. ..	91
Carburetter	S.U. type HS2
Needle: Standard	AN
Rich	H6
Weak	EB
Fuel pump	S.U. type L

Rear axle

		Optional
Rear axle ratio	4·22 : 1	4·55 : 1
Overall gear ratios:		
First	15·28 : 1	16·51 : 1
Second	9·17 : 1	9·88 : 1
Third	5·95 : 1	6·42 : 1
Top	4·22 : 1	4·55 : 1
Reverse	19·66 : 1	21·22 : 1

Tyres

Sizes	5·20—14 cross-ply
	145—14 radial-ply

Pressures:

	Cross-ply	Radial-ply
Fully equipped, 2 up:		
Front	22 lb./sq. in. (1·6 kg./cm.²)	24 lb./sq. in. (1·7 kg./cm.²)
Rear: Saloon	22 lb./sq. in. (1·6 kg./cm.²)	26 lb./sq. in. (1·8 kg./cm.²)
Traveller	24 lb./sq. in. (1·7 kg./cm.²)	
Fully equipped, 4 up:		
Front	22 lb./sq. in. (1·6 kg./cm.²)	
Rear	24 lb./sq. in. (1·7 kg./cm.²)	

GENERAL DATA

Electrical

Polarity	Positive earth (+)

Battery

Types: Lucas	D9, DZ9; A9, AZ9 or A7, AZ7
Capacities (at 20 hr. rate)	40 amp.hr. or 30 amp.hr.

Dimensions:

Track:		Saloon	Traveller
Front	.. ..	50⅝ in. (1·284 m.)	50⅝ in. (1·284 m.)
Rear ..	.. ..	50 5/16 in. (1·278 m.)	50 5/16 in. (1·278 m.)
Turning circle:			
Right-hand ..	..	33 ft. 1 in. (10·09 m.)	33 ft. 1 in. (10·09 m.)
Left-hand ..	..	32 ft. 11 in. (10·04 m.)	32 ft. 11 in. (10·04 m.)
Toe-in ..	.. ..	3/32 in. (2·4 mm.)	3/32 in. (2·4 mm.)
Wheelbase ..	..	7 ft. 2 in. (2·185 m.)	7 ft. 2 in. (2·185 m.)
Length (overall)	..	12 ft. 4 in. (3·76 m.)	12 ft. 5 in. (3·78 m.)
Width (overall)..	..	5 ft. 1 in. (1·55 m.)	5 ft. 1 in. (1·55 m.)
Height (overall)	..	5 ft. 0 in. (1·52 m.)	5 ft. 0½ in. (1·53 m.)
Ground clearance	..	6¾ in. (17·14 cm.)	6¾ in. (17·14 cm.)

Weights

Kerbside weight:

2-door	.. ..	1,686 lb. (764 kg.)	1,821 lb. (826 kg.)
4-door	.. ..	1,733 lb. (786 kg.)	
Convertible ..	..	1,688 lb. (766 kg.)	
Towing weight (max.)		1,680 lb. 762 kg.)	1,680 lb. (762 kg.)

Capacities:

Fuel tank	6½ gallons (29·6 litres)
Cooling system..	8¾ pints (5 litres)
Heater (when fitted)	1 pint (·57 litre)
Engine sump	6½ pints (3·69 litres) (including filter)
Gearbox	2¼ pints (1·3 litres) engine oil
Rear axle	1½ pints (·85 litre) Hypoid oil

CONTROLS AND INSTRUMENTS

Hand brake

Pulling the lever upwards operates the rear wheel brake-shoes mechanically. Release the brake by pulling on the lever to take the load and then pressing on the ratchet release with the thumb before pushing the handle downwards into the 'off' position.

Pedals

The pedals are arranged in the orthodox positions—namely, the clutch pedal, brake pedal, and accelerator, reading from left to right. Do not drive with your foot resting on the clutch pedal. It is bad practice and leads to rapid clutch wear. Make sure that the clutch pedal has the necessary free movement before it engages the withdrawal mechanism (see page 44).

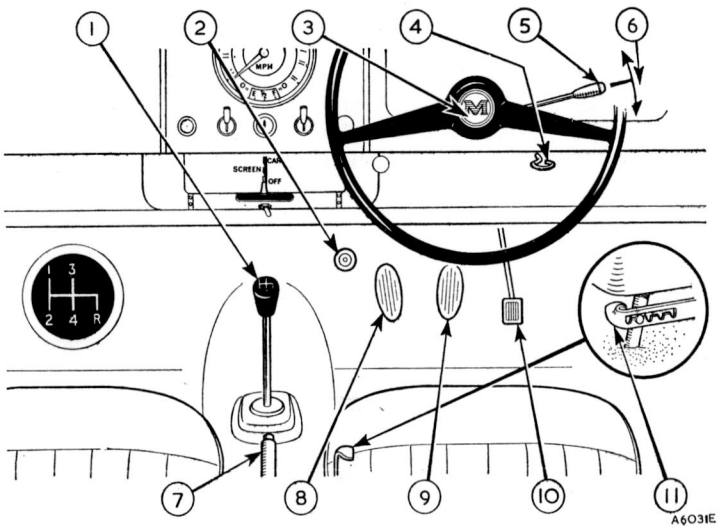

The driving controls

1. Gear lever.
2. Headlight dip switch.
3. Horn-push.
4. Bonnet lock release.
5. Direction indicator warning light.
6. Direction indicator switch.
7. Hand brake.
8. Clutch pedal.
9. Brake pedal.
10. Accelerator.
11. Seat adjustment.

Gear lever

First and second gears are selected by moving the lever to the left and engaged by moving it forward for first gear or backwards for second gear. Third and fourth gears are selected by moving the lever to the right through the neutral position till resistance is felt, then forward for third gear and backwards for fourth gear.

To engage reverse gear, move the lever to the right in the neutral position until resistance is felt, apply further side pressure to overcome the resistance, and then move it backwards to engage the gear. Synchromesh engagement is provided on second, third, and fourth gears.

CONTROLS AND INSTRUMENTS

Headlight beam dipping switch and warning light

The headlight beam dipping switch is situated in the centre of the toeboard. It is of the single-acting repeating type, dipping the light beams on one depression and raising the beams on the next depression.

A warning light on the instrument dial glows when the headlight beams are in the raised position.

Horn switch

The horn is sounded by pressing the centre disc of the steering-wheel.

Direction indicators

The direction indicators are operated (when the ignition is switched on) by a switch lever fitted on the steering-column.

On R.H.D. models the switch lever is moved upwards to operate the left-hand indicators and downwards to operate the right-hand indicators.

On L.H.D. models upward movement operates the right-hand indicators, and downward movement the left-hand indicators.

A warning lamp in the end of the lever flashes when the indicators are operating. Should one of the indicator bulbs 'fail', the remaining bulb and warning lamp will flash with increased frequency.

Seat adjustment

The driver's seat is adjustable and is secured in position by a spring-loaded lever which extends beyond the front of the seat and must be depressed when moving the seat forward or backward.

When the lever is released it automatically engages its stop to lock the seat in position.

If the range of adjustment is insufficient to suit drivers of exceptional stature the seat may be repositioned on the floor of the car.

Bonnet release

Release the bonnet lock from inside the car by a pull on the control ring which is to be found under the instrument panel on the extreme right-hand side of the parcel tray.

The bonnet is still retained by the safety hook, which must be released as indicated on page 14.

Choke or mixture control

Pull out the control to assist starting when the engine is cold; the fuel/air mixture will be progressively enriched as the control is pulled out. Always use the minimum setting for the shortest possible time and push the control in completely as soon as the engine will run without its use.

Approximately the first $\frac{1}{4}$ in. (6 mm.) of movement opens the throttle slightly giving a fast idling speed without affecting the mixture.

CONTROLS AND INSTRUMENTS

Ignition and starter switch

The ignition and starter are controlled by a single switch and a removable key which also locks the door(s). To switch on the ignition, insert the key and turn it in a clockwise direction until a slight resistance is felt. Further movement in the same direction operates the starter motor. Release the key immediately the engine starts. If the engine fails to start first time wait until it has come to rest before using the starter again.

The continued use of the starter when the engine fails to start will discharge the battery.

If the pinion fails to disengage when the engine starts, the starter will emit a high-pitched whine and the engine must be stopped immediately.

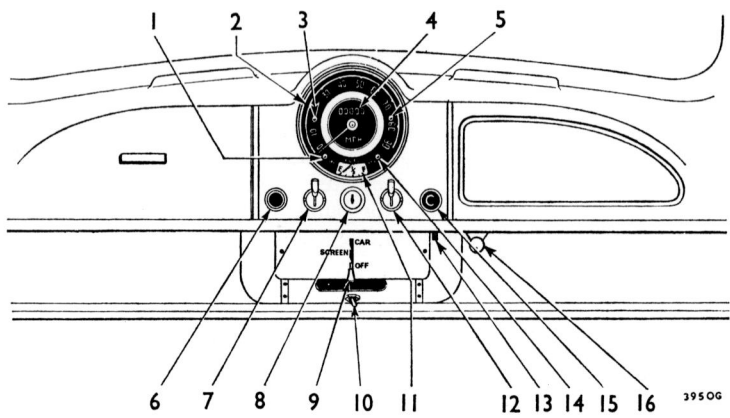

The instruments and switches

1. Headlight main-beam warning light.
2. Speedometer.
3. Oil filter warning light (when fitted).
4. Total mileage.
5. Oil pressure warning light.
6. Windscreen washer.
7. Windscreen wiper switch.
8. Ignition and starter switch.

9. Air distribution shutter lever.
10. Heater switch.
11. Fuel gauge.
12. Lighting switch.
13. Panel light switch.
14. Ignition warning light.
15. Mixture control.
16. Heater control valve.

Ignition warning light

The ignition warning light serves the dual purpose of reminding the driver to switch off the ignition before leaving the vehicle and of acting as a no-charge indicator. The light should glow with the ignition switched on and at a slow idling speed. As the engine speed increases, the light should dim and eventually go out. On cars equipped with an alternator the warning light should go out immediately the engine has started. If the light does not go out, an incorrectly adjusted or broken fan belt, or other fault in the charging system, is indicated.

CONTROLS AND INSTRUMENTS

Lighting switch

The head, side, and tail lights are controlled by a lever-type switch; move the lever downwards to the half-way position for the side and tail lights, and into the fully down position for headlights.

Details of replacement bulbs are given on page 38.

Panel light switch

Switch on by moving the lever to the left. (The light can only be used when the pilot lights are on.)

The correct replacement bulb is indicated on page 38.

Windscreen wiper switch

Move downwards to operate the wipers, with the ignition switched on.

The blades park automatically when switched off.

Windscreen washer

To wash the screen, press the pump control button. When following other vehicles, particularly under dirty road conditions, the washer should be used before the wiper blades are switched on.

In cold weather the reservoir should be filled up with a mixture of water and one of the recommended washer solvents to prevent the water freezing on the windscreen. **Do not use radiator anti-freeze in the washer.**

Roof lamp switch

The lever-type switch is fitted in the base of the lamp body. In addition, automatic switches are fitted to the two front pillars; opening either front door will switch on the roof light.

Heater

Comprehensive instructions on the use of the heater are given on pages 10 and 11.

Fuel gauge

A few seconds after the ignition is switched on the fuel gauge, which is incorporated in the instrument dial, indicates the quantity of fuel in the tank. See page 20 for notes on **'Filling up with fuel'.**

Oil pressure warning light

This glows when the ignition is switched on and fades out after the engine has started. Low oil pressure or insufficient oil in the sump is indicated by the light glowing when the engine is running. If the light continues to glow while there is enough oil in the sump, switch off immediately and have the lubricating system checked by an authorized Distributor or Dealer.

Oil filter warning light (when fitted)

The oil filter warning light, which is incorporated in the instrument dial, is a guide to the need for a more frequent oil and filter element change. For full details see page 56.

Later models are not fitted with an oil filter switch and although the amber lens may be fitted there is no connection from the filter.

HEATING AND VENTILATION

Heater (earlier models)

Some de-luxe models are fitted with heating and ventilating equipment consisting of a circular radiator, below the fascia, which is provided with hot water from the engine cooling system and is equipped with an air-circulating fan.

The heating system has three controls:

(1) A rheostat switch on the heater unit which controls the motor for the circulating fan.

(2) A screw-down valve on the rear of the cylinder head which closes the water circulation.

(3) A fresh-air intake control, positioned below the parcel shelf.

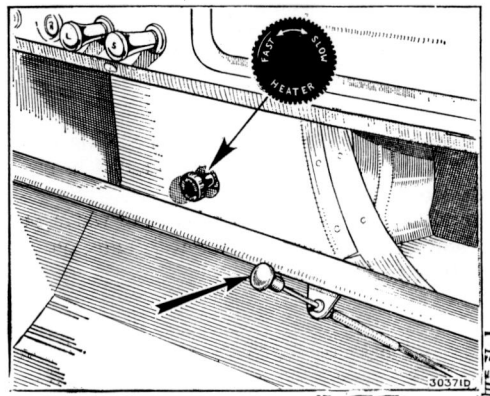

The switch for the heater circulating fan and the fresh-air intake control (earlier models)

The screw-down water valve (earlier models)

The blower motor will run only while the ignition is switched on. The first few degrees of movement of the switch will run the motor at maximum speed. Further turning of the switch knob will gradually reduce the speed of the fan to regulate the quantity of air delivered to the car interior.

With the air intake control pushed in, fresh air is excluded from the intake duct and air is drawn from the interior of the car only for heating and re-circulation. When the control is pulled out fresh air will be ducted into the heater from the exterior of the car.

Close the screw-down valve on the engine if a general circulation of fresh air is required in warm weather.

See 'FROST PRECAUTIONS' on page 25.

Heater (later models)

This has the blower motor incorporated in the heater box. Three controls are used:

(1) An air distribution shutter lever.

(2) A blower motor switch.

(3) A valve on the rear of the cylinder head, controlling the flow of coolant to the heater.

The heater controls (later models)

1. Air distribution shutter lever.
2. Blower motor switch.
3. Heater control valve.

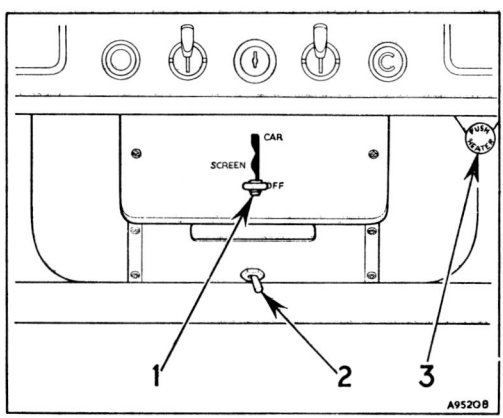

Heater control valve

Push in the heater control valve knob on the fascia if a circulation of heated air is required.

Air distribution

The lever projecting from the front face of the heater box at its centre controls the air distribution shutter and can be set in any one of three positions.

When set in the top (CAR) position air is distributed to the interior of the vehicle. In the centre (SCREEN) position air is directed onto the windscreen.

The supply of air is cut off when the lever is in the lowest (OFF) position.

Blower motor and switch

The blower motor greatly increases the supply of air to the heater unit, and thus the volume of heat or fresh-air output.

The blower should be switched on when maximum performance from the heating or ventilating system is required or to compensate for the lack of ram effect at the air intake when the vehicle is travelling at low speed.

The switch for the blower is located on the lower edge of the switch panel at its centre and will only operate when the ignition is switched on.

NOTE.—Should unpleasant fumes be drawn in from outside, switch off the blower motor and set the shutter operating lever in the 'OFF' position until outside conditions improve.

See 'FROST PRECAUTIONS' on page 25.

BODY

Interior

Clean the carpets with a semi-stiff brush or vacuum cleaner, preferably before washing the outside of the car. The most satisfactory way to give carpets a thorough cleaning is with Decosol Interior Cleaner, diluted with an equal quantity of water. Apply vigorously with a semi-stiff brush, and remove the surplus with a damp cloth or sponge. Carpets should not be cleaned by the 'dry-clean' process. The upholstery and roof lining may be treated with undiluted Decosol Interior Cleaner spread thinly over the surface to be cleaned with a 1 in. (25 mm.) brush or cloth. Leave for five minutes, then wipe off with a moist sponge or cloth.

Decosol can be used for cleaning and renovating all the usual upholstery materials and rubber, but it should not be used on painted surfaces.

Coachwork

Regular care of the body finish is necessary if the new appearance of the car exterior is to be maintained against the effects of air pollution, rain, and mud.

Wash the bodywork frequently, using a soft sponge and plenty of water containing a mild detergent. Large deposits of mud must be softened with water before using the sponge. Smears should be removed by a second wash in clean water, and with the sponge if necessary. When dry, clean the surface of the car with a damp chamois-leather.

In addition to the regular maintenance, special attention is required if the car is driven in extreme conditions such as sea spray, or on salted roads. In these conditions and with other forms of severe contamination an additional washing operation is necessary which should include underbody hosing.

Any damaged areas should be immediately covered with paint and a complete repair effected as soon as possible. Before touching in light scratches and abrasions with paint thoroughly clean the surface. Use petrol/white spirit (gasoline/hydrocarbon solvent) to remove spots of grease or tar.

The application of BMC Car Polish is all that is required to remove traffic film and to ensure the retention of the new appearance.

Bright trim

Never use an abrasive on stainless, chromium, aluminium, or plastic bright parts and on no account clean them with metal polish. Remove spots of grease or tar with petrol/white spirit (gasoline/hydrocarbon solvent) and wash frequently with water containing a mild detergent.

When the dirt has been removed polish with a clean dry cloth or chamois-leather until bright. Any slight tarnish found on stainless or plated components which have not received regular washing may be removed with BMC Chrome Cleaner. An occasional application of mineral light oil or grease will help to preserve the finish, particularly during winter when salt may be used on the roads, but these protectives must not be applied to plastic finishes.

Windscreen

Windscreen smearing can be removed with BMC Screen Cleaner.

Care of varnish on exterior woodwork

Wash regularly with water to which a suitable detergent has been added.

Thoroughly dry the varnish afterwards, paying particular attention to the joints in the woodwork.

Re-varnish the woodwork annually, using the method and a varnish as recommended by your Distributor or Dealer.

Sand the original varnish with 320 grade wet-and-dry paper, used dry.

The approved products mentioned are obtainable from your Distributor/Dealer.

To operate the interior door handles of the four-door saloon pull or push them to the positions indicated— (1) rear door and (2) front door

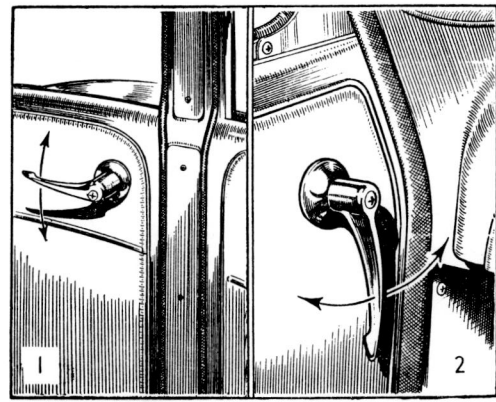

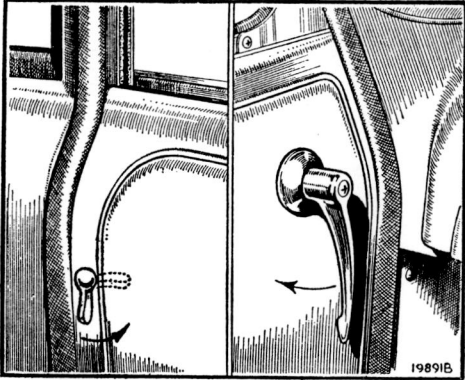

The passenger's door of the Traveller and two-door saloon is locked by operating the small lever located on the edge of the door. Turn the lever anti-clockwise to lock

Door locks

Four-door saloon

The driver's door, right- or left-hand drive, is lockable with the ignition key. To lock the remaining doors from inside, push the front handles forward and the rear door handles downwards.

Two-door saloon

Both doors are lockable with the ignition key, and a safety catch is provided on the passenger's door; this is turned anti-clockwise to the horizontal position to lock.

Traveller (rear door)

The rear doors are held in the closed position by two bolt rods actuated by a single handle, which is turned clockwise to release the doors.

The doors are locked by inserting the Yale-type key provided into the centre of the handle and turning the key anti-clockwise.

BODY

Opening the bonnet

Unlock the bonnet by pulling the control ring located under the right-hand side of the fascia panel.

Release the safety hook by depressing the lever underneath the bonnet near the centre.

Raise the bonnet lid until the bonnet prop trips into engagement and supports the bonnet. Make sure the prop is correctly engaged before working under the bonnet.

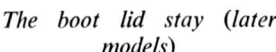

Fold the Traveller seat cushion and back squab as indicated to provide a loading platform

The boot lid stay (later models)

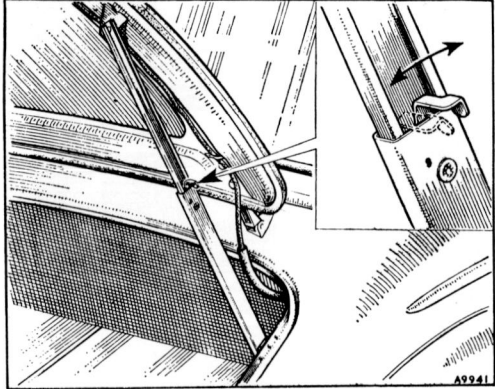

Closing the bonnet

Raise the bonnet and release the prop, then lower the bonnet to engage the safety hook. Apply double hand pressure to force the bonnet down into the fully closed position. The bonnet lock will be heard to spring into engagement.

It is important to keep the bonnet lock properly oiled.

Folding seat (Traveller)

When required, the rear seat can be folded downwards to provide a flat loading platform. To fold the seat raise the seat cushion into the vertical position

14

by the hand-pulls, and then fold the seat back downwards after releasing the two sliding bolts which retain it in position on the body side rails.

Luggage compartment

A spacious luggage compartment is provided in the boot with a separate compartment for the spare wheel and tools. As the boot lid is raised the support stay springs into engagement and holds it in the open position. To close, raise the lid slightly, press the lever on the support stay rearwards to release the locking catch, and lower the lid. The boot can be locked with the separate key provided.

After releasing the hood fold it upwards and backwards

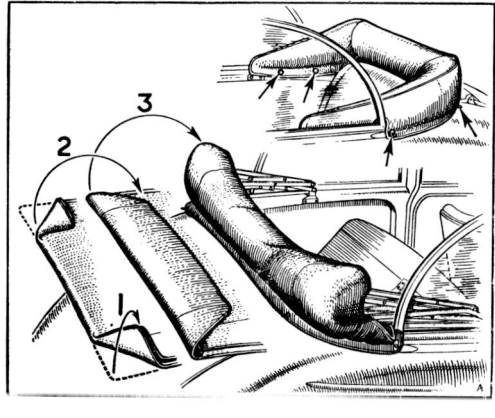

Fold the hood and secure it with the hood cover and press studs

Raising the hood (Convertible)

When raising the hood ensure that the overlap at the edge of the hood cloth embraces the window frame, particularly at the curve of the quarter-light.

Folding the hood

To release the hood on Convertible models unscrew the two wing bolts attaching the forward end of the hood to the head rail. The hood can be raised upwards and backwards into the position illustrated.

BODY

By pulling on the hood members at the positions shown the hood can be folded so that the hood sticks lie on top of each other, care being taken that the hood material is not trapped.

Draw the hood material rearwards clear of the sticks so that it is free from creases and fold the corners over as shown at (1). Then fold it in half as shown at (2), finally rolling it over the hood sticks as shown at (3).

Stowing the hood

Fit the hood cover over the folded hood and fasten it in position with the press studs as shown.

Care of the hood

Cleaning should be carried out with soap and warm water on the exterior only; detergents should not be used.

The hood should never be folded wet, but allowed to dry erected.

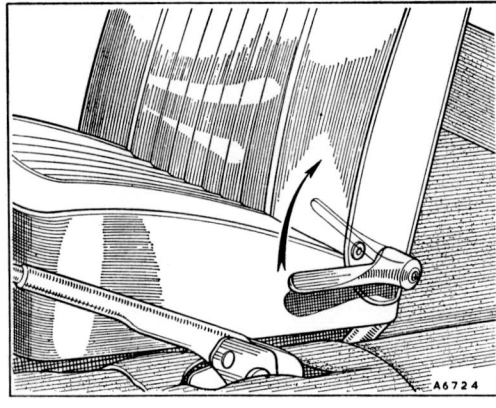

The reclining front seat operating lever

Reclining front seats (when fitted)

The angle of the front seat back-rest can be adjusted by means of the lever on the inside of each seat.

Roof rack

The roof rack must be regarded as a means of carrying bulky rather than heavy articles of luggage, i.e. articles which, by virtue of their shape or size, cannot be stowed conveniently inside the vehicle. Any weight carried on the roof will have an adverse effect on the handling of the vehicle, which must be driven with due discretion. A straight ride will not be effected to any great degree, although cornering and behaviour in a cross-wind will be different due to the change in position of the centre of gravity and the centre of pressure.

Weight in excess of 50 lb. (23 kg.) should not be carried on the roof.

SEAT BELTS

Seat belts are obtainable from Distributors and Dealers and should be fitted only by them to attachment points incorporated in the car body. No alterations or additions must be made to the belts.

Two types of belt, i.e. 'static' and 'automatic', are available for front seat use. The belt must be adjusted until the buckle is located at the side of the hip (see illustration).

Ensure that the short front seat belt used is on the side of the tunnel away from the user.

Always wear lap-and-diagonal belts as a complete assembly.

Always ensure that the belt is lying flat and is not twisted either on the wearer's body or between the wearer and the anchorage point. Never at any time wear a belt loosely as this reduces its protection.

Never attempt to use the seat belt for more than one person, even for small children. When a belt is not in use, ensure that it is stowed correctly.

If the seat belts have had to withstand the strain of a severe impact they must be replaced.

A static seat belt showing the correct position of the buckle

The following instructions apply to the recommended seat belts available from your Distributor or Dealer.

Front seats

Static

To fasten, lift the magnetic buckle tongue and engage the hook with the hinged part of the tongue.

To release, lift the buckle tongue.

To adjust, move the adjuster on the long belt until the lap belt is comfortably tight and the diagonal belt passes over the chest, with flat hand clearance.

To stow, hook the long belt onto the door pillar parking device.

SEAT BELTS

Automatic

The diagonal portion of the belt is free and movement of the wearer's body is unrestricted unless the car brakes or corners hard, when the reel locks the belt immediately.

To fasten, push the tongue into the buckle until it is locked, indicated by a positive click.

To release, lift the front plate of the buckle while keeping a slight body pressure against the belt.

To adjust, move the tongue on the long belt until the lap portion is comfortably tight.

To stow, move the tongue on the long belt towards the door pillar pulley bracket.

Care of the belts

Do not attempt to bleach the belts webbing or re-dye it. If the belts become soiled, sponge with warm water using a non-detergent soap and allow to dry naturally. **Do not use caustic soap, chemical cleaners or detergents for cleaning; do not dry with artificial heat or by direct exposure to the sun.**

Inspect the belt webbing periodically for signs of abrasion or wear, paying particular attention to the fixing points and adjusters.

If at any time the webbing is unthreaded from the brackets and adjuster, ensure that it is re-threaded correctly.

RUNNING INSTRUCTIONS

Before running the engine, carry out the preliminaries indicated below.

Filling the cooling system

The radiator should be filled to approximately $\frac{1}{2}$ in. (13 mm.) below the bottom of the filler neck.

Unscrew the filler cap slowly if it is being removed while the engine is hot. Protect your hand against escaping steam.

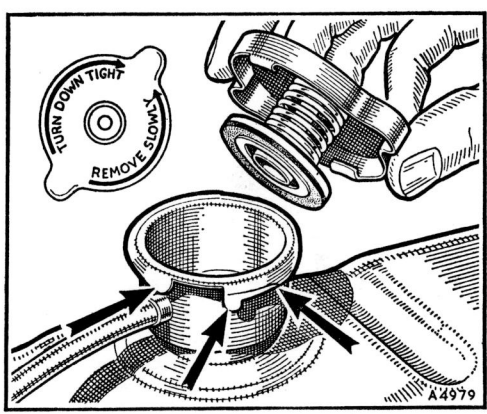

Press the cap downwards and turn anti-clockwise to release the radiator cap The system operates at 4 p.s.i. (0·28 kg./cm.²) and the cap is marked with a figure 4

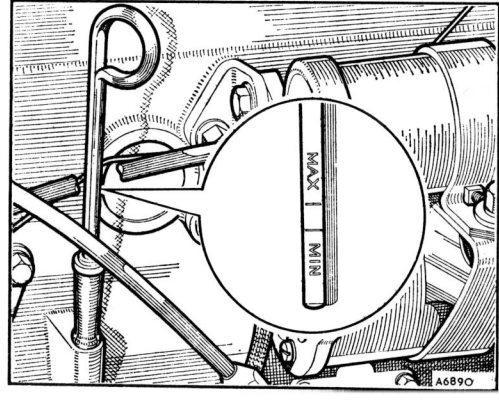

The engine oil level dipstick is located on the right-hand side of the crankcase block

Checking the engine oil level

Check the supply of oil in the sump weekly by withdrawing the dipstick on the right-hand side of the crankcase block. Wipe the lower portion of the rod, reinsert it, and withdraw it again. Oil will cling to the rod and show the level of oil in the sump.

The correct oil level is indicated by the 'MAX' mark on the dipstick, and the oil should be maintained at this level.

RUNNING INSTRUCTIONS

Filling up with engine oil
The filling orifice is situated on top of the rocker cover and it has a quick-action cap. Fill up with correct grade of oil (see 'RECOMMENDED LUBRICANTS' page 66).

Tyre pressures
The tyre pressures should be checked and, if necessary, adjusted weekly. The correct tyre pressures are given on page 4.

Filling up with fuel
When filling up with fuel avoid filling the tank until fuel is visible in the filler intake tube. Should this be done and the car left in the sun, there will be a considerable risk of fuel leakage due to expansion, and consequent danger from exposed fuel. If inadvertently overfilled, take care to park the car in the shade with the filler intake as high as possible.

Starting up
Check that the gear lever is in the neutral position and the hand brake is applied. Set the choke control, as necessary, and operate the starter (see page 7).

Warming up
Run the engine fairly fast at approximately 1,000 r.p.m. which corresponds to a speed of 16 m.p.h. (26 km.p.h.) in top gear, so that it attains its correct working temperature as quickly as possible. Do not allow the engine to idle slowly as this leads to excessive cylinder wear and far less damage will be done by driving the vehicle straight onto the road from cold. Return the choke control as soon as the engine will run without its use.

Induction heaters (when fitted)
A carburetter induction heater* is fitted to vehicles in countries where conditions of extreme cold exist. This heater is thermostatically controlled and is brought into operation below 4° C. (40° F.) when the ignition is switched on. Wait four minutes between switching on the ignition and operating the starter control to allow the heater to warm up from a temperature of —10° C. (14° F.); allow proportionately shorter times for higher temperatures up to 0° C. (32° F.). Never leave the ignition switch on for longer than the recommended periods with the engine at rest.

NOTE.—To relieve the extra load on the ignition switch it is important that all auxiliary services wired through the switch are switched off before stopping the engine.

Running-in speeds
The treatment given to a new car will have an important bearing on its subsequent life, and engine speeds during this early period must be limited. The following instructions should be strictly adhered to.

During the first 500 miles (800 km.)
DO NOT exceed 45 m.p.h. (72 km.p.h.).
DO NOT operate at full throttle in any gear.
DO NOT allow the engine to labour in any gear.

* Suction chamber heater also fitted to early units.

WHEELS AND TYRES

Tyre pressures

On new cars the spare wheel is inflated above the recommended pressure and it must be checked and adjusted before use.

Maintain the tyre pressures of all tyres including the spare to the figures given in 'GENERAL DATA'. Check with an accurate tyre gauge at least once a week. Any unusual pressure loss should be investigated. Under-inflation causes rapid tyre wear, and even more serious is the possible damage to the cords of the fabric owing to excessive flexing of the cover walls.

Tyre valves

The air-tightness of the valve depends upon the proper functioning of its interior. It may be tested for air-tightness by rotating the wheel until the valve is at the top and inserting its end in water. If bubbles appear the seating is faulty and should be removed. It should be replaced by a new one.

Always ensure that the valve interiors are screwed well home and valve caps are tightened.

Tyre care

Excessive local distortion as a result of striking a kerb, a loose brick, a deep pot-hole, etc., may cause the casing cords to fracture. Every effort should be made to avoid such obstacles.

Any oil or grease which may get onto the tyres should be cleaned off by using petrol (fuel) sparingly. Do not use paraffin (kerosene), which has a detrimental effect on rubber.

Flints and other sharp objects should be removed with a penknife or similar tool. If neglected, they may work through the tyre.

Penetration does not normally result in deflation of a tubeless tyre if the object is not pulled out; the tyre should be repaired when convenient. Penetrations by objects of small diameter can be repaired with the tyre manufacturer's plugging kit.

NOTE.—The insertion of a plug to repair a puncture in a tubeless tyre must be regarded as a temporary measure and **a permanent vulcanized repair must be made as soon as possible.**

Tubeless tyres

Tubeless tyres are identified by the word 'tubeless' on the sidewall. A self-sealing rubber valve is pressed into the wheel as (3) in the illustration.

Radial-ply tyres

Radial-ply tyres should only be fitted in sets of four although in certain circumstances it is permissible to fit a pair on the rear wheels; tyres of different construction must not be used on the same axle. A pair must never be fitted to the front wheels with conventional tyres at the rear.

Consult your Distributor or Dealer before changing to radial-ply tyres.

WHEELS AND TYRES

Tyre wear

To obtain the maximum mileage from your set of tyres occasionally inter-change the front and rear wheels, and bring the spare into use. Your Distributor or Dealer will advise you of the most suitable time.

Changing the position of wheels is only recommended for vehicles fitted with standard cross-ply tyres. When radial-ply tyres are fitted they must be retained on the axle and in the position in which they were balanced.

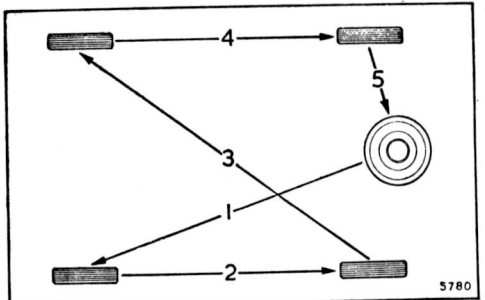

Cross-ply tyres only. Interchange the road wheels in this order to bring the spare wheel into use

Remove the rubber plug from the jacking socket and insert the lifting arm of the jack

Spare wheel and jack

The spare wheel is carried in the luggage boot of the Saloon and Convertible models and beneath the rear loading platform on the Traveller. It is secured in position by a clamp plate and released when required by unscrewing the clamp holding bolt. Stow the jack between the fuel filler spout and the spare wheel.

Look at the jack occasionally, clean off accumulated dust, and lightly oil the thread to prevent the formation of rust. If the jack is neglected it may be difficult to use in a roadside emergency.

WHEELS AND TYRES

Jack operation

Apply the hand brake.

Remove the rubber plug from the socket located on either side beneath the door pillar and insert the arm of the special jack. As the car will swing over when one side is raised the base of the jack should be positioned slightly inwards at the start of the lift so that it is vertical when the wheels are clear of the ground.

Removing the wheel discs

Remove a wheel disc by inserting the cranked end of the special lever between the road wheel and the edge of the disc; lever the disc away from the wheel with a sideways motion. To refit the hub disc the rim should be placed over two of the protrusions on the wheel centre and the outer face given a sharp blow with the fist over the third protrusion.

Removing a hub disc

Removing the wheels

Slacken the four nuts securing the road wheel to the hub. Raise the car to lift the wheel clear of the ground and remove the nuts. Withdraw the road wheel from the hub. When replacing the road wheel, refit the securing nuts with the taper side towards the wheel. Make certain that the nuts are tight, but at the same time avoid overtightening. The recommended torque figure is 37 to 39 lb. ft. (5·1 to 5·4 kg. m.).

Removing and fitting tyres

Inextensible wires are incorporated in the tyre beads. Do not attempt to stretch the beads over the rim. Force is entirely unnecessary and dangerous and will damage the bead. Fitting or removing is quite easy if the wire beads are carefully adjusted into the rim base. If the cover bead fits tightly on the rim seating it should be freed by using the tyre levers.

As the bead forms the air seal in the wheel rim great care must be taken not to damage the bead; use tyre levers in good condition.

Initial inflation can be carried out with a tyre pump and tourniquet but more easily with an air-line.

COOLING SYSTEM

Filling the cooling system

The radiator should be filled to approximately ½ in. (13 mm.) below the bottom of the filler neck. The coolant should be an anti-freeze solution or water containing a corrosion inhibitor.

Unscrew the filler cap slowly if it is being removed while the engine is hot. Protect your hand against escaping steam.

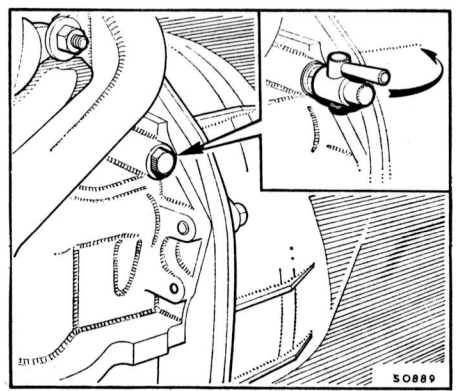

The cylinder block drain plug is located on the left-hand side at the rear. Inset: Tap fitted to earlier units, turn in direction of arrow to open

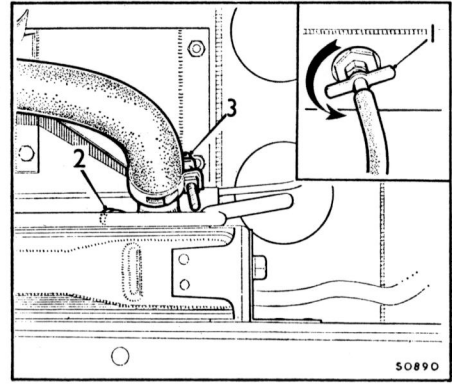

Radiator draining points
1. Tap fitted to earlier units, turn in direction of arrow to open.
2. Plug (when fitted).
3. Bottom hose.

Draining the cooling system

Remove the radiator filler cap, the drain plug from the rear left-hand side of the engine and the drain plug from the base of the radiator; when the radiator is not fitted with a drain plug release the bottom hose at the radiator. Collect the coolant in a clean container if it contains anti-freeze and is required for re-use.

COOLING SYSTEM

Frost precautions

Water expands when it freezes, and if precautions are not taken there is considerable risk of bursting the radiator, cylinder block or heater. The heater unit cannot be drained with the cooling system and it is therefore essential to use anti-freeze in the cooling system in freezing conditions.

When freezing conditions are likely to be encountered, have the specific gravity of the coolant checked by your Distributor or Dealer, and add anti-freeze to give the required protection. After the second year the system should be drained and flushed by inserting a hose in the filling orifice and allowing water to flow through until clean. Make sure the cooling system is watertight, examine all joints and change any defective hose for a new one. Refill with the appropriate anti-freeze solution.

Only anti-freeze of the ethylene-glycol type incorporating the correct type of corrosion inhibitor is suitable and owners are recommended to use Bluecol Anti-freeze. We also approve the use of any anti-freeze that conforms to Specification B.S.3151 or B.S.3152.

The degrees of frost resistance given by anti-freeze solutions to engines fitted with heaters are as follows:

Anti-freeze (%)	Commences to freeze		Frozen solid		Amount of anti-freeze		
	°C.	°F.	°C.	°F.	Pts.	U.S. pts.	Litres
25	—13	9	—26	—15	$2\frac{1}{2}$	3	1·4
33⅓	—19	—2	—36	—33	$3\frac{1}{4}$	4	1·8
50	—36	—33	—48	—53	5	6	2·8

Do not use radiator anti-freeze solution in the windscreen-washing equipment. Use the correct washer solvent, which will not damage the paintwork.

ELECTRICAL EQUIPMENT

Fuses

The main fuses are housed in a separate fuse block.

Fuse marked 'A1' and 'A2' protects the accessories which are connected so that they operate irrespective of whether the ignition is on or off.

Fuse marked 'A3' and 'A4' protects the accessories which are connected so that they operate only when the ignition is switched on.

The line fuse for the pilot and tail lights is located in the cylindrical tube situated in the wiring loom beneath the regulator. To renew the fuse hold one end of the tube, push in, twist, and pull off the other end. The fuse is then accessible.

Spare fuses are provided and it is important to use only the correct replacement fuse. The fusing value is marked on a coloured paper slip inside the glass tube of the fuse.

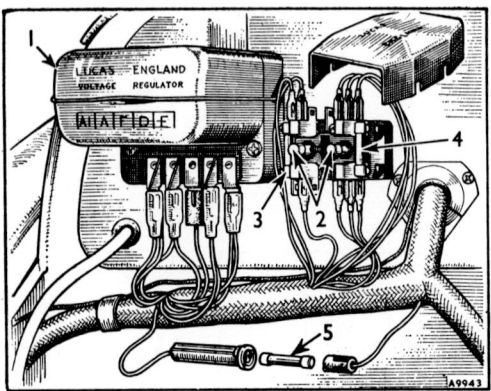

The regulator and fuses
(later models)

1. Regulator cover.
2. Spare fuses.
3. 'AUX.' fuse (35-amp.).*
4. 'AUX. IGN.' fuse (35-amp.).*
5. Side and tail light fuse.

Voltage regulator

This is a sealed unit, located on the engine bulkhead, controlling the charging rate of the dynamo in accordance with the needs of the battery. The regulator requires no attention and should not be disturbed.

Coil

The coil requires no attention beyond keeping its exterior clean, particularly between the terminals.

High-tension cables

When renewing ignition cables on earlier vehicles, fill the holes in the distributor cap with silicone grease and push the cables well into the holes in the cap before tightening the securing screws. Later cars are fitted with plug-in type cables and sealing sleeves.

Jammed starter pinion

In the event of the starter pinion becoming jammed in mesh with the flywheel, it can usually be freed by turning the starter armature by means of a spanner applied to the shaft extension at the commutator end.

* Blow rating.

Windscreen wiper

The windscreen wiper is controlled by a switch on the fascia. The blades park automatically when switching off.

No adjustment or lubrication is necessary as the gears are packed with grease on assembly.

To reposition a blade, remove it and refit it on a different spline as shown.

To ensure that the windscreen is wiped as clean as possible, the blade rubbers should be renewed each year. The blade can be released from the wiper arms by lifting the retaining clip.

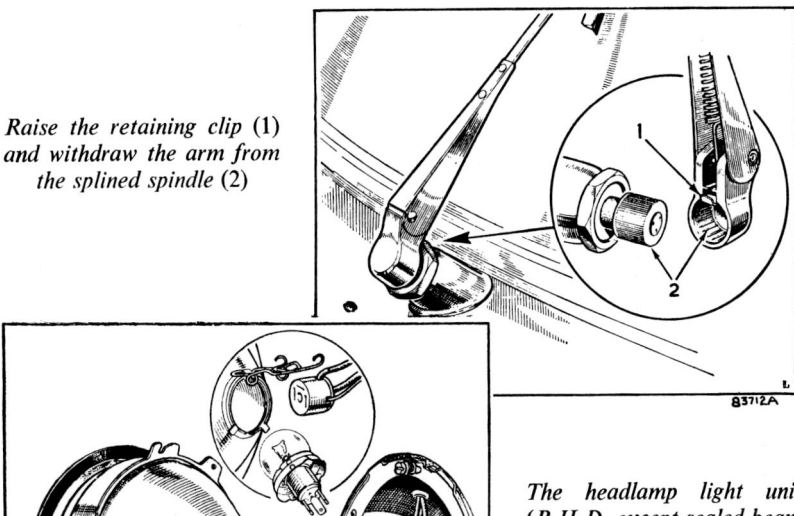

Raise the retaining clip (1) and withdraw the arm from the splined spindle (2)

The headlamp light unit (R.H.D. except sealed-beam type) removed, showing the bulb holder and back-shell, etc., with the European type lamp shown inset

Headlamps (European type)

To renew the headlamp bulb remove the screw from beneath the headlamp and withdraw the rim. Remove the three inner rim retaining screws and the rim and pull the light unit forward from the back-shell.

Early cars: Press the light unit and turn anti-clockwise to release it from the back-shell.

The bulb is released by withdrawing the three-pin socket and pinching the two ends of the wire retaining clip to clear the bulb flange. When replacing the bulb care must be taken to see that the rectangular pip on the bulb flange engages the slot in the reflector seating. Replace the spring clip with its coils resting in the base of the bulb flange and engaging the two retaining lugs on the reflector seating for the bulb.

27

ELECTRICAL EQUIPMENT

Headlamps (R.H.D. except sealed-beam type)

Access to the bulb is obtained in the same manner as that described for European-type headlamps. Twist the back-shell anti-clockwise and pull it off. The bulb can then be withdrawn from its holder.

The U.K. sealed-beam head-lamp with the beam-adjusting screws indicated by the arrows

The North American sealed-beam headlamp with the beam-adjusting screws indicated by the arrows

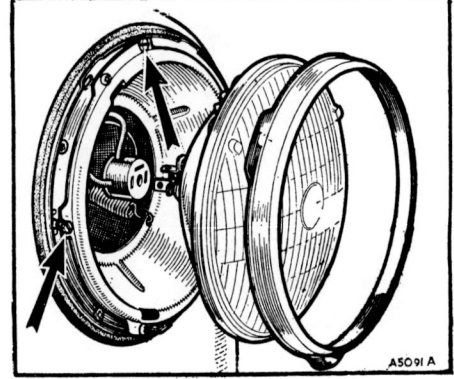

Headlamps (U.K. sealed-beam type)

To change a sealed-beam light unit remove the lamp rim by releasing the rim retaining screw at the bottom of the rim assembly. Remove the three retaining screws securing the inner lamp rim and remove the rim assembly. Pull the unit forward and disconnect the three-pin socket to release it from the back-shell.

Headlamps (North American sealed-beam type)

To change a sealed-beam light unit remove the retaining screw from the bottom face of the lamp rim and detach the rim. Slacken the three Phillips screws securing the light unit retaining rim and turn the rim anti-clockwise to remove, supporting the lens of the light unit at the same time. Pull off the three-pin plug from the rear of the light unit.

Setting the headlight beams

The headlight beams must be set so that the main driving beams are straight ahead and parallel with each other and $\frac{1}{2}°\pm\frac{1}{4}°$ below horizontal, or in accordance with local regulations.

To adjust, remove the lamp rim and set the lamp to the correct position in the vertical plane by turning the adjusting screw at the top of the light unit in a clockwise direction to raise and anti-clockwise to lower the beam. Horizontal adjustment is made by turning the adjustment screw on the right-hand side of the light unit. Some early units have an adjusting screw on each side of the light unit.

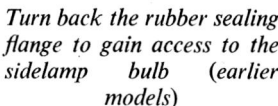

Turn back the rubber sealing flange to gain access to the sidelamp bulb (earlier models)

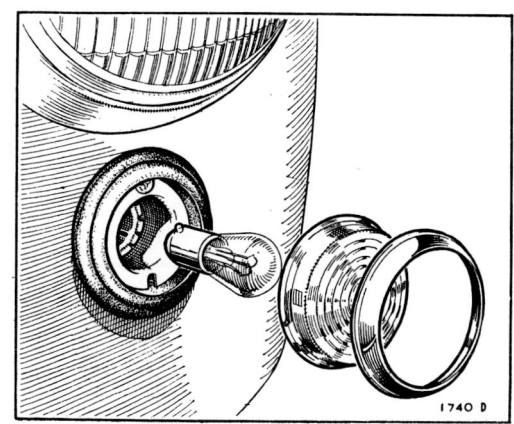

1740 D

Sidelamps and front direction indicator lamps (earlier models)

Access to the sidelamp bulb for replacement is obtained by folding back the rubber flange and removing the plated rim and lamp glass. Only the fingers should be used to fold back the rubber flange.

The sidelamps are also the flashing direction indicators and the bulb-locating pins are offset to ensure correct replacement of the bulbs.

Sidelamps and front direction indicator lamps (later models)

To obtain access to either bulb press the lamp front inwards and turn it anti-clockwise until it is free to be withdrawn. Reverse this movement to replace the front.

Both bulbs are of the bayonet-type fixing.

ELECTRICAL EQUIPMENT

Stop, tail, and rear direction indicator lamps (earlier Saloon and Convertible)

Access to the tail lamp bulb is obtained by withdrawing the two screws to release the lamp cover.

The bulbs are of the double-filament type, giving a marked increase in illumination on brake application to provide a stop warning.

The bulb-locating pins are offset to ensure correct replacement of the bulbs.

The side and flasher lamp with the lens removed to show the four lens-retaining catches on the lamp body (later models)

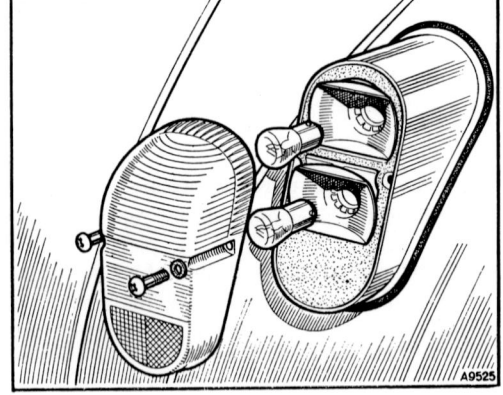

Remove the two screws to gain access to the rear lamp bulbs (later Saloon and Convertible)

Stop, tail, and rear direction indicator lamps (later Saloon and Convertible)

Access to the bulbs is obtained by withdrawing the two screws holding the lens cover. Ensure that the rubber washers are refitted on replacement.

Stop, tail, and rear direction indicator lamps (later Traveller)

To remove the bulbs for replacement, fold back the rubber flange and withdraw the plated rim and lamp glass. Only the fingers should be used to fold back the rubber flange.

Number-plate lamp

The number-plate lamp operates only when the sidelamps and tail lamps are switched on. Access to the bulb is obtained by unscrewing the slotted screw to release the domed cover.

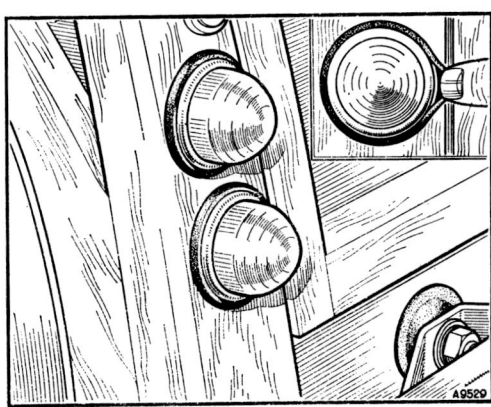

Turn back the rubber sealing flanges to gain access to the lamp bulbs. The upper (amber) lamp is the flashing indicator (later Traveller)

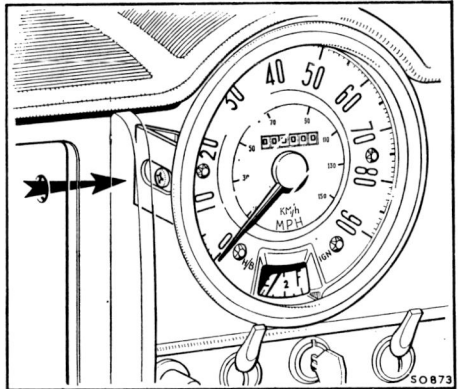

Insert a screwdriver through the hole in each glovebox to engage and release the instrument securing screws

Panel and warning lights

Access to the warning lights for ignition, headlight beam, oil pressure and oil filter is effected by removing the central combined instrument, which is held in position by two captive screws. A hole will be seen in the inner wall of each glovebox through which the captive screws, one on each side of the instrument can be reached with a screwdriver.

The instrument draws out forwards, and defective bulbs can then easily be replaced.

A list of replacement bulbs will be found on page 38.

WIRING DIAGRAM

For pre-1965 models which have a relay in the flasher unit

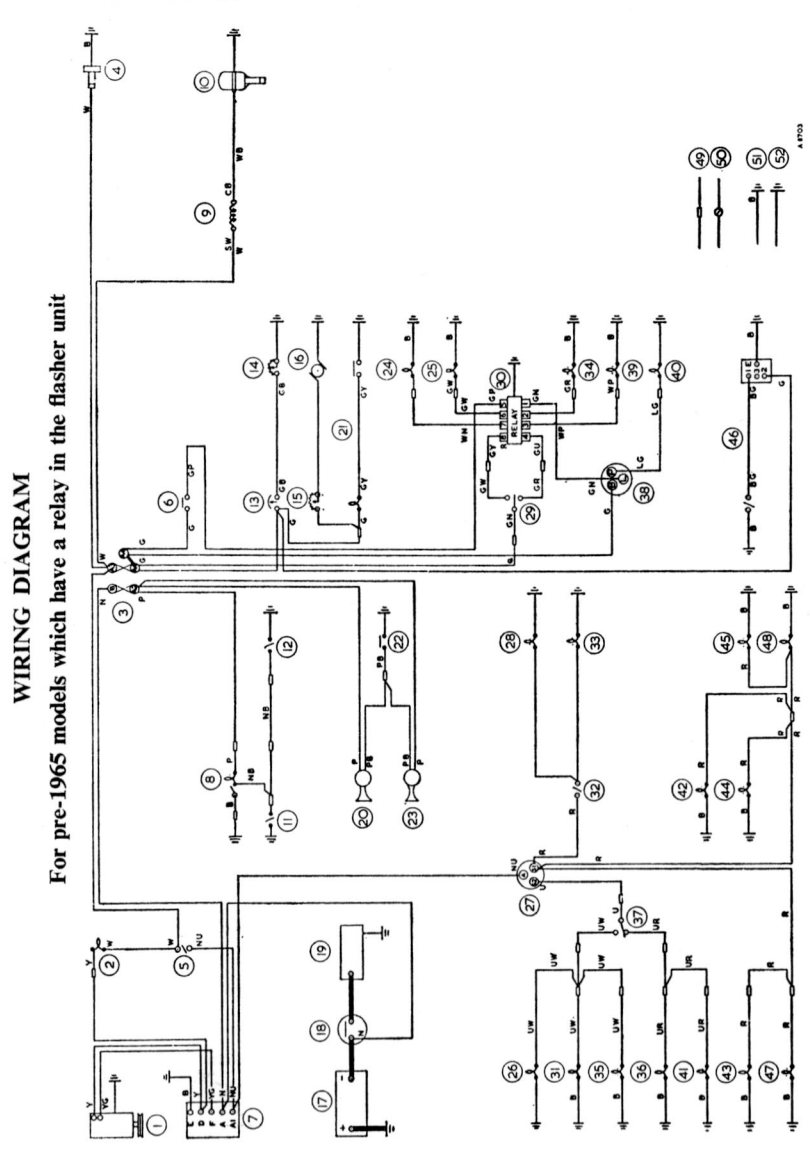

KEY TO WIRING DIAGRAM

For pre-1965 models which have a relay in the flasher unit

1. Dynamo.
2. Ignition warning light.
3. Fuse unit.
4. Fuel pump.
5. Ignition switch.
6. Stop lamp switch.
7. Control box.
8. Interior light and switch (when fitted)—earthed to control box terminal 'E'.
9. Ignition coil.
10. Distributor.
11. Courtesy light switch (when fitted).
12. Courtesy light switch (when fitted).
13. Fuel gauge.
14. Fuel tank unit.
15. Heater rheostat (when fitted).
16. Heater (when fitted).
17. 12-volt battery.
18. Starter switch.
19. Starter motor.
20. Horn.
21. Oil pressure warning light and switch.
22. Horn push.
23. Horn.
24. R.H. rear flasher and stop lamp.
25. R.H. front flasher.
26. Main-beam warning light.
27. Lighting switch.
28. Panel light.
29. Flasher switch.
30. Relay—flashers.
31. R.H. headlight main beam.
32. Panel light switch.
33. Panel light.
34. L.H. front flasher.
35. L.H. headlight main beam.
36. ¶R.H. headlight dip beam.
37. Dipper switch.
38. Flasher unit.
39. L.H. rear flasher and stop lamp.
40. Flasher warning light.
41. L.H. headlight dip beam.
42. R.H. tail lamp.
43. L.H. side lamp.
44. L.H. tail lamp.
45. Number-plate lamp.
46. Screen wiper switch and motor—earthed to control box terminal 'E'.
47. R.H. side lamp.
48. Number-plate lamp.
49. Snap connectors.
50. Terminal blocks or junction box.
51. Earth connections made via cable.
52. Earth connections made via fixing bolts.

NOTE.—Twin number-plate lamps fitted to Traveller models only.

CABLE COLOUR CODE

B.	Black.	P.	Purple.	Y.	Yellow.
U.	Blue.	R.	Red.	D.	Dark.
N.	Brown.	S.	Slate.	L.	Light.
G.	Green.	W.	White.	M.	Medium.

When a cable has two colour code letters the first denotes the main colour and the second denotes the tracer colour.

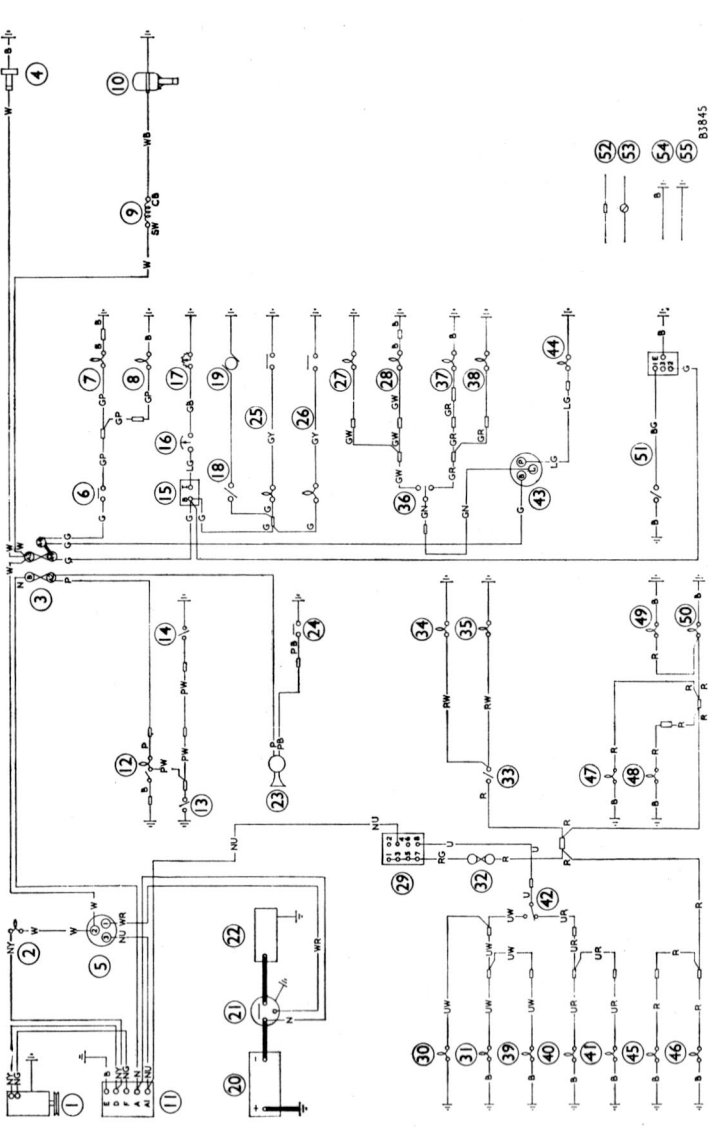

WIRING DIAGRAM

B3845

KEY TO WIRING DIAGRAM

1. Dynamo.
2. Ignition warning light.
3. Fuse unit.
4. Fuel pump.
5. Ignition and starter switch.
6. Stop lamp switch.
7. R.H. stop lamp.
8. L.H. stop lamp.
9. Ignition coil.
10. Distributor.
11. Control box.
12. Interior light and switch (when fitted).
13. Courtesy light switch (when fitted).
14. Courtesy light switch (when fitted).
15. Instrument voltage stabilizer.
16. Fuel gauge.
17. Fuel tank unit.
18. Heater switch (when fitted).
19. Heater (when fitted).
20. 12-volt battery.
21. Starter solenoid switch.
22. Starter motor.
23. Horn.
24. Horn-push.
25. Oil filter warning light and switch (when fitted).
26. Oil pressure warning light and switch.
27. R.H. front flasher.
28. R.H. rear flasher.
29. Lighting switch.
30. Main-beam warning light.
31. R.H. headlamp main beam.
32. Line fuse (10-amp.).
33. Panel light switch.
34. Panel light.
35. Panel light.
36. Flasher switch.
37. L.H. rear flasher.
38. L.H. front flasher.
39. L.H. headlamp main beam.
40. R.H. headlamp dip beam.
41. L.H. headlamp dip beam.
42. Dipper switch.
43. Flasher unit.
44. Flasher warning light.
45. L.H. side lamp.
46. R.H. side lamp.
47. R.H. tail lamp.
48. L.H. tail lamp.
49. Number-plate lamp.
50. Number-plate lamp.
51. Windscreen wiper switch and motor—earthed to control box terminal 'E'.
52. Snap connectors.
53. Terminal blocks or junction box.
54. Earth connections made via cable.
55. Earth connections made via fixing bolts.

NOTE.—Twin number-plate lamps fitted to Traveller models only.

CABLE COLOUR CODE

B. Black.
U. Blue.
N. Brown.
G. Green.
P. Purple.
R. Red.
S. Slate.
W. White.
Y. Yellow.
D. Dark.
L. Light.
M. Medium.

When a cable has two colour code letters the first denotes the main colour and the second denotes the tracer colour.

WIRING DIAGRAM
(Alternator-equipped Vehicles)

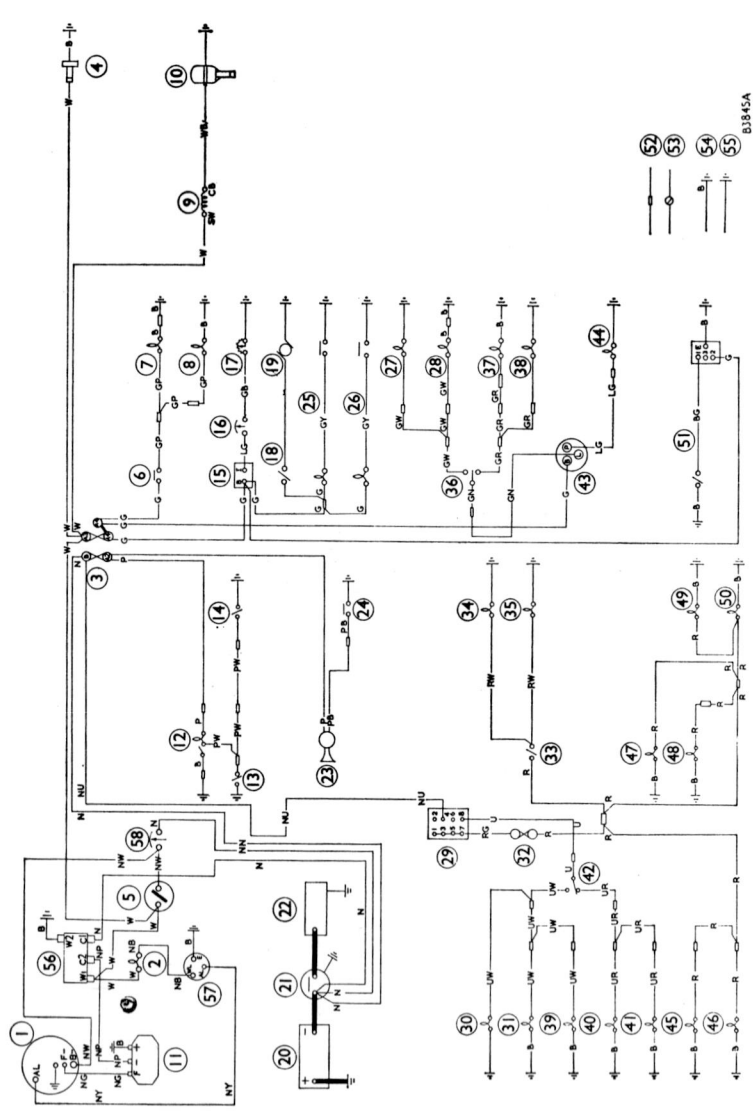

KEY TO WIRING DIAGRAM
(Alternator-equipped Vehicles)

1. Alternator.
2. Charging warning light.
3. Fuse unit.
4. Fuel pump.
5. Ignition and starter switch.
6. Stop lamp switch.
7. R.H. stop lamp.
8. L.H. stop lamp.
9. Ignition coil.
10. Distributor.
11. 4TR control unit.
12. Interior light and switch (when fitted).
13. Courtesy light switch (when fitted).
14. Courtesy light switch (when fitted).
15. Instrument voltage stabilizer.
16. Fuel gauge.
17. Fuel tank unit.
18. Heater switch (when fitted).
19. Heater (when fitted).
20. 12-volt battery.
21. Starter solenoid switch.
22. Starter motor.
23. Horn.
24. Horn-push.
25. Oil filter warning light and switch (when fitted).
26. Oil pressure warning light and switch.
27. R.H. front flasher.
28. R.H. rear flasher.
29. Lighting switch.
30. Main beam warning light.
31. R.H. headlamp main beam.
32. Line fuse (10-amp.).
33. Panel light switch.
34. Panel light.
35. Panel light.
36. Flasher switch.
37. L.H. rear flasher.
38. L.H. front flasher.
39. L.H. headlamp main beam.
40. R.H. headlamp dip beam.
41. L.H. headlamp dip beam.
42. Dipper switch.
43. Flasher unit.
44. Flasher warning light.
45. L.H. side lamp.
46. R.H. side lamp.
47. R.H. tail lamp.
48. L.H. tail lamp.
49. Number-plate lamp.
50. Number-plate lamp.
51. Windscreen wiper switch and motor—earthed to control box terminal 'E'.
52. Snap connectors.
53. Terminal blocks or junction box.
54. Earth connections made via cable.
55. Earth connections made via fixing bolts.
56. 6RA relay.
57. 3AW warning light unit.
58. Ammeter.

CABLE COLOUR CODE

B. Black.   P. Purple.   Y. Yellow.
U. Blue.   R. Red.   D. Dark.
N. Brown.   S. Slate.   L. Light.
G. Green.   W. White.   M. Medium.

When a cable has two colour code letters the first denotes the main colour and the second denotes the tracer colour.

ELECTRICAL EQUIPMENT

Roof lamp

The roof lamp is operated by a switch provided on the forward edge of the lamp itself.

Access to the bulb for replacement is achieved by first removing the two screws on the plastic lamp cover and then the cover.

Alternator-equipped vehicles

The following precautions must be observed to prevent inadvertent damage to the alternator and its control equipment.

1. Ensure that all electrical connections in the generating and charging circuit are maintained tight at all times.
2. Do not run the engine with the battery or any of the charging circuit cables disconnected. If for any reason the engine is to be run with the charging circuit incomplete, disconnect the car wiring cables from the alternator and wire the main terminals together using an external bridging wire.
3. Ensure that the correct battery polarity is maintained at all times, Positive or Negative as indicated by the battery earth connection.
4. If electric arc-welding equipment or a boost (high-rate) battery charger is to be used on the car, all electric cables must be disconnected from the alternator and control box terminals.

Heated rear window (where fitted)

The later type of window has the heating element on the surface of the glass and with reasonable care will last indefinitely. The following practices will damage the circuit and must be avoided.

1. Scratching off labels and advertising stickers.
2. Wiping the glass with the back of a ringed hand.
3. Stowing hard and metal objects so that they abrade the glass.
4. Cleaning with harsh abrasives.

Replacement bulbs

	Watts	Part No.
Headlamps, R.H.D.	50/40	BFS 414
Headlamps, Europe (except France—dip vertical) ..	45/40	GLB 410
Headlamps, France (dip vertical)	45/40	BFS 411
Sidelamps	6	GLB 989
Sidelamps with direction indicators (earlier models) ..	6/21	GLB 380
Direction indicators, front and rear (later models) ..	21	GLB 382
Tail and stop lamps	6/21	GLB 380
Number-plate lamp (single bulb)	6	GLB 989
Number-plate lamp (twin bulbs)	4	BFS 222
Panel and warning lights	2·2	GLB 987
Roof lamp	6	GLB 989
Roof lamp (alternative festoon type)	6	GLB 254
Direction indicator warning light (Lilliput)	1·5	GLB 280

IGNITION

Static ignition timing

The point where ignition should start is given in 'GENERAL DATA'. With the crankshaft stationary at this position the contact breaker points should be just beginning to open. When the engine is running, timing is varied by a centrifugal advance mechanism and a vacuum control.

Checking static ignition timing

The following information describes a method of checking the ignition timing; it does not detail the resetting of the timing when the distributor has been removed from the engine.

The groove in the crankshaft pulley and the pointers to assist correct timing. The long pointer indicates T.D.C. The arrow (far right) indicates the vernier adjusting nut on the distributor

Check that the contact points are set to the correct gap when the cam follower is on one of the peaks of the distributor cam (see page 48).

The rim of the crankshaft pulley has a small groove which will correspond with the long pointer on the timing cover when Nos. 1 and 4 pistons are at T.D.C. The other two pointers indicate 5° and 10° B.T.D.C. Turn the crankshaft with the starting-handle until the groove in the pulley is in the correct position (see 'GENERAL DATA').

With the crankshaft in this position the contact points should be just about to open.

If the points are open, turn the knurled nut (see illustration) towards 'R' until they are closed. If the points are closed, turn the knurled nut towards 'A'. In either case, turn the nut until the points are just parting.

A simple electrical method may be used to ensure an accurate check. Connect a 12-volt bulb between the low-tension terminal on the side of the distributor and a good earth point on the engine. Switch on the ignition. If the bulb lights, turn the knurled nut towards 'R' until the light goes out and then back towards 'A' until it just lights: this will give the correct static timing.

If this adjustment cannot be made with the knurled nut, consult your Distributor/Dealer.

CARBURETTER ADJUSTMENT

Carburetter slow-running adjustment

When the engine is fully run in the slow-running may require adjustment. This should be done when the engine has attained its normal running temperature. If the slow-running speed only (not mixture strength) needs correction, this can be made on the throttle adjusting screw (2) by turning it clockwise to increase and anti-clockwise to decrease the engine speed.

If however, the engine beat is uneven, denoting irregular firing, the mixture strength may need adjustment—but remember that defective compression, a faulty valve, or faulty ignition may also cause misfiring.

After the slow-running has been adjusted check the fast-idle adjustment by pulling out the mixture control knob on the fascia (a minimum of $\frac{1}{4}$ in. or 6 mm.) until the linkage is about to move the carburetter jet, and adjust the fast-idle adjusting screw (3) to give an engine speed of about 1,000 r.p.m. when hot.

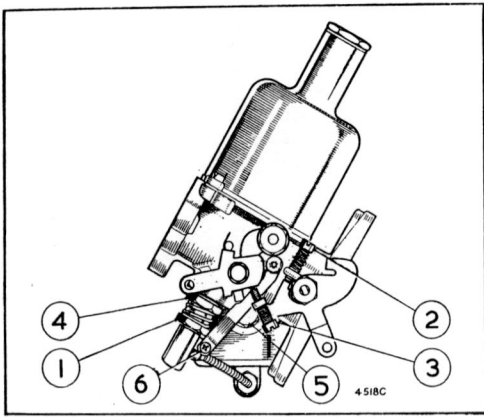

The carburetter

1. Jet adjusting nut.
2. Throttle adjusting screw.
3. Fast-idle adjusting screw.
4. Jet locking nut.
5. Float-chamber securing bolt.
6. Jet link securing screw.

Carburetter jet adjustment

Uneven firing can be caused by a mixture which is too weak; the exhaust beat then is uneven with a splashy or irregular type of misfire, and the exhaust is colourless. Uneven firing can also be caused by a mixture which is too rich; the misfire is then of a rhythmical or regular type, coupled with a blackish exhaust.

According to the symptoms, screw the jet adjusting nut (1), only one flat of the hexagon at a time, either upwards to weaken or downwards to enrich the mixture until the fastest idling speed is obtained consistent with even firing.

Under no circumstances should the jet locking nut (4) be slackened as this will cause misalignment of the main jet, resulting in the jamming of the piston.

When adjusting the mixture strength it may be helpful if the idling speed of the engine is increased by about half a turn of the throttle adjusting screw, which must be suitably reduced when the correct mixture strength has been obtained.

When the mixture and slow-running speed are satisfactory the remainder of the throttle range will also be correct.

MAINTENANCE ATTENTION

The recommended lubricants are indicated on page 66.

Every 3,000 miles (5000 km.) or 3 months

Engine oil level and coolant level—see page 19.

Carburetter damper lubrication

Every 3,000 miles (5000 km.) remove the damper unit and pour oil into the hollow piston rod to a point $\frac{1}{2}$ in. (13 mm.) above the top of the rod. Under no circumstances should a heavy-bodied lubricant be used.

Failure to lubricate the piston damper will cause the piston to flutter and reduce acceleration.

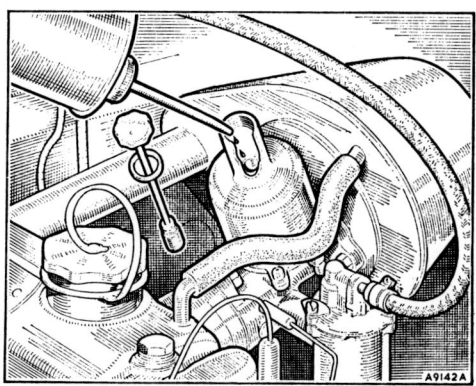

Lubricating the carburetter damper (10MA engine shown)

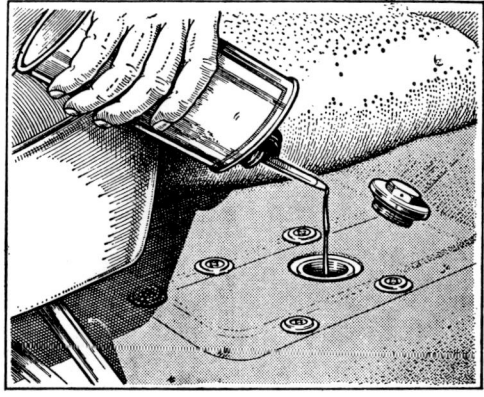

Unscrew the reservoir cap to inspect the hydraulic fluid level. Clean thoroughly before replacing

Topping up the master cylinder with hydraulic fluid

Every 3,000 miles (5000 km.) the brake fluid level must be checked by turning back the front floor carpet on the driver's side and removing the exposed filler plug. The fluid level should be $\frac{1}{2}$ in. (13 mm.) below the bottom of the filler neck and must never be above it. Replenish if necessary.
Use only Lockheed Brake Fluid (Series 329), or a fluid to specification S.A.E. J1703a (Grade 1).

41

Every 3,000 miles (5000 km.) or 3 months

Brake adjustment

Adjustment is necessary when excessive travel of the brake pedal takes place on application.

Chock the wheels which remain in contact with the ground. Use the special jack and raise each side of the car in turn (see page 22).

Front brakes

Remove the front wheel and rotate the brake-drum until one of the adjustment screws is visible through the hole provided in the brake drum. With a screwdriver turn the screw as far as it will go in a clockwise direction until the drum is locked solid, then turn the screw anti-clockwise **one** notch only. The brake-drum should then be free to rotate without the shoes rubbing.

Turn the drum until the adjustment screw diametrically opposite is visible and carry out the same procedure on this. The brake-shoes on this wheel are now fully adjusted. The brake-shoes on the other front wheel must be adjusted by the same method.

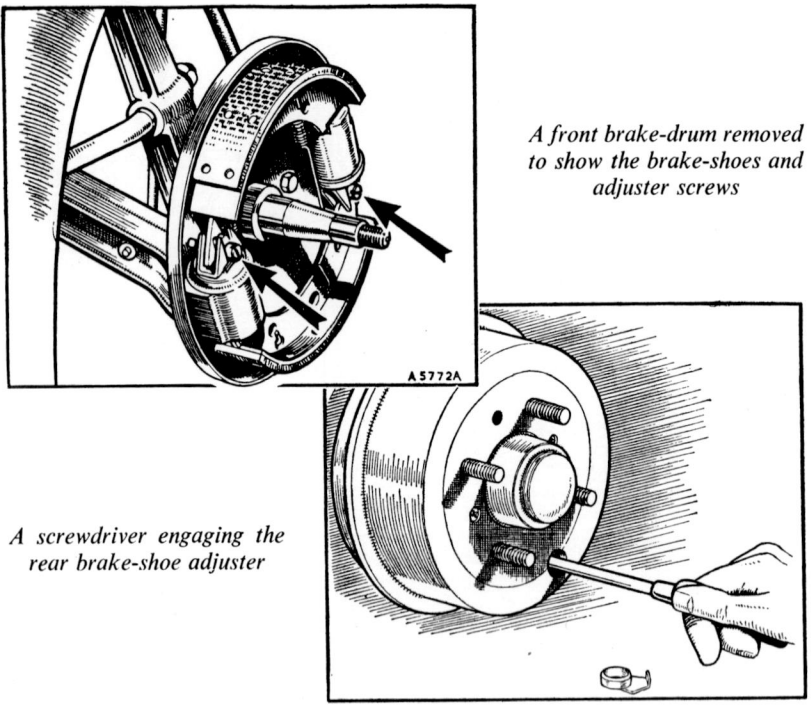

A front brake-drum removed to show the brake-shoes and adjuster screws

A5772A

A screwdriver engaging the rear brake-shoe adjuster

Rear brakes

The procedure is similar to that detailed for the front brakes except that there is only one adjuster for both brake shoes.

It is essential that the hand-brake should be fully released while the rear brake-shoes are being adjusted.

Do not forget to replace the sealing plug in the hole in the brake-drum.

Hand brake

The hand brake operates on the shoes in the rear brake-drums and is automatically adjusted when the hydraulic brake adjustment is made. Consult your Distributor or Dealer if hand brake travel is excessive *after brake adjustment has been carried out.*

Hand brake cables

Every 3,000 miles (5000 km.) a grease gun filled with grease should be applied to the grease nipples on the hand brake cables and given three or four strokes.

Propeller shaft

The two needle-type universal joints should be lubricated every 3,000 miles (5000 km.).

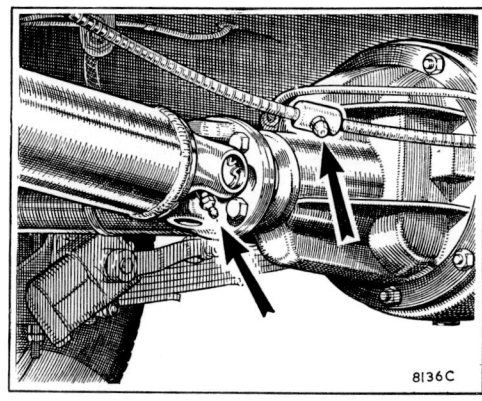

The propeller shaft rear universal joint and the brake cable lubricating nipples

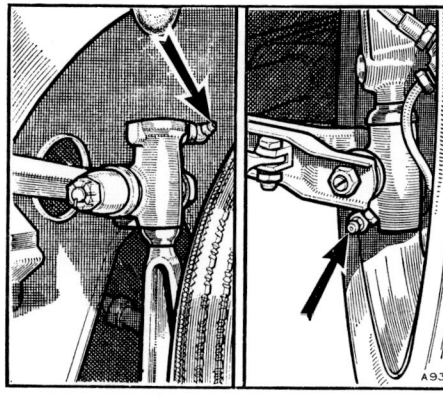

The lubricating nipples on the upper and lower swivel pin links

Swivel pins

Nipples are provided at the top and bottom of each swivel pin. A grease gun should be filled with grease and applied to the nipples every 3,000 miles (5000 km.).

Three or four strokes of the gun should be given, and where the car is used in dusty conditions more frequent lubrication is recommended.

Every 3,000 miles (5000 km.) or 3 months

Steering tie-rod

Every 3,000 miles (5000 km.) a gun filled with grease should be applied to the nipples on the ends of the steering tie-rods and given three or four strokes.

The inner ball joints of the tie-rods (those within the rubber boots) are automatically lubricated from the steering-rack housing.

The lubricating nipple on the steering tie-rod

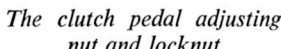

The clutch pedal adjusting nut and locknut

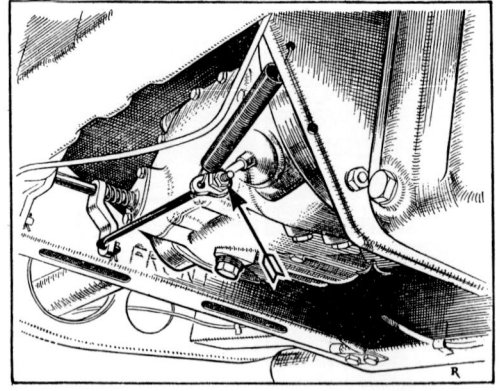

Clutch pedal clearance

There must always be free movement of $1\frac{3}{8}$ in. (35 mm.) to $1\frac{1}{2}$ in. (38 mm.) at the pedal pad. Check and adjust as necessary.

Do not forget to tighten the locknut.

Every 3,000 miles (5000 km.) or 3 months

Battery topping-up

The battery must be kept clean and dry, and the terminals should be smeared with petroleum jelly.

In hot weather or when long journeys are to be made the electrolyte levels may require topping-up more frequently than as recommended in the 'MAINTEN-ANCE SUMMARY'. When checking the electrolyte in the cells **do not use a naked light** and see that the vehicle is standing level. Do not use tap water for topping-up.

Type D9 or DZ9. Remove the manifold and check the level of the electrolyte in each cell. These levels must be maintained so that the separator guard is just covered; top up with distilled water as necessary. Do not overfill. After topping-up wipe the top of the battery dry (refer to illustration on page 50).

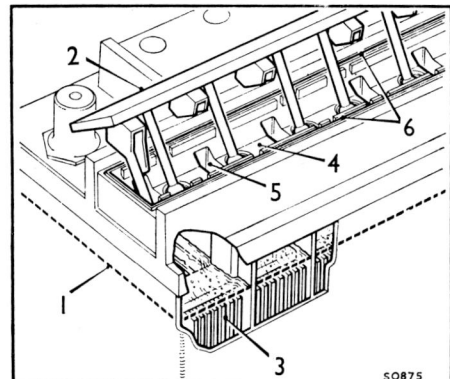

The Lucas A9 battery

Type A9 ('Pacemaker'). Inspect the level of the electrolyte (1) in each cell either by looking through the translucent battery case, or after lifting the vent cover (2) vertically and tilting it to one side when fully raised; topping-up is not necessary unless the electrolyte is below the tops of the plates (3) in any cell. If topping-up is required, pour distilled water into the trough (4) until all the rectangular filling slots (5) are full and the bottom of the trough is just covered. Wipe away any surplus from the cover seating grooves (6) and refit the cover firmly, which automatically distributes the correct amount of water to each cell.

Topping-up should not be carried out within half an hour of the battery having been charged, other than by the vehicle's own generating system, lest it floods. In extremely cold conditions run the engine immediately after topping-up so as to mix the electrolyte.

Important.—The vent cover must be kept closed at all times, except when topping-up. The electrolyte will flood if the cover is raised while either trickle- or fast-charging the battery. Fast charging should only be undertaken in extreme circumstances, and must not exceed 40 amps. for a maximum period of one hour. A single-cell heavy discharge tester cannot be used on this type of battery. On no occasion should the vent cover be detached from the battery.

For a complete summary of the 3,000 miles (5000 km.) or 3 months service refer to page 57.

Every 6,000 miles (10000 km.) or 6 months

Dynamo belt adjustment

It should be possible to deflect the belt $\frac{1}{2}$ in. (13 mm.) at the longest run. Adjust by slackening all the bolts supporting the unit and pivot inwards or outwards, as necessary, using hand pressure.

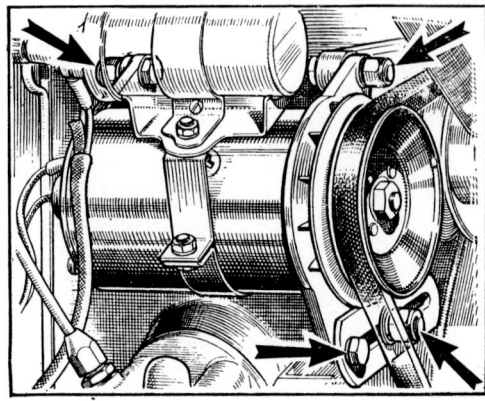

The dynamo attachment points to be slackened for belt adjustment

The engine sump drain plug located on the right-hand side of the engine

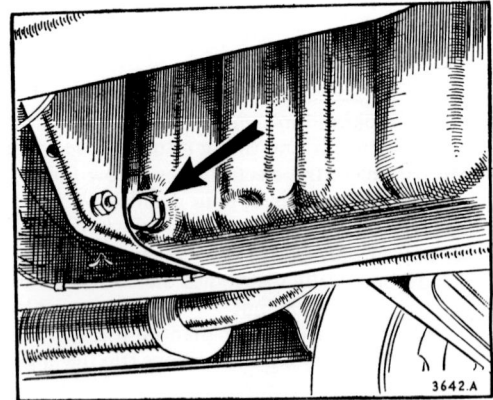

Draining the engine sump

We recommend that the sump should be drained every 6,000 miles (10000 km.) if using multigrade oil. Remove the hexagon-headed plug from the right-hand side of the sump and allow the oil to drain, preferably when the oil is warm. Clean the plug, refit, and refill the sump with one of the recommended lubricants.

Every 6,000 miles (10000 km.) or 6 months

Oil filter

The engine oil filter element must be renewed every 6,000 miles (10000 km.). Unscrew the central retaining bolt to release the filter bowl and element.

Clean the filter bowl thoroughly before refitting and make certain that the correct replacement is obtained for the make of filter fitted.

Make certain that the seating washer is in good order; it must be renewed should there be any doubt as to its condition. Ensure that the bowl is refitted correctly, and the retaining bolt tightened to 16 lb. ft. (2·2 kg. m.).

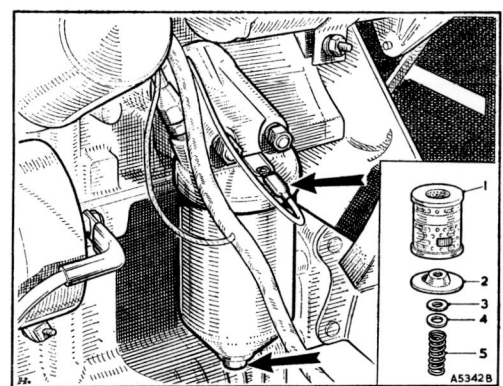

The engine oil filter, showing the warning light pressure differential switch lead (when fitted) and filter retaining bolt

1. Filter element.
2. Seating plate.
3. Seating washer.
4. Steel washer.
5. Spring.

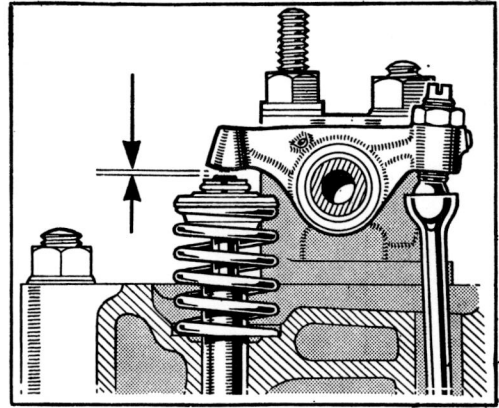

Slacken the locknut and rotate the screw clockwise to reduce and anti-clockwise to increase the valve rocker clearance

Valve rockers

The valve rocker clearances should be checked every 6,000 miles (10000 km.), and adjusted where necessary to have a clearance between the rocker arm and the valve stem of at least ·012 in. (·30 mm.) when cold.

Adjustment must be made with the tappet on the back of the cam. Testing and adjustments should be carried out in the following order:

No. 1 valve with No. 8 fully open.   No. 8 valve with No. 1 fully open.
No. 3   ,,   ,, No. 6 ,,   ,,   No. 6   ,,   ,, No. 3   ,,   ,,
No. 5   ,,   ,, No. 4 ,,   ,,   No. 4   ,,   ,, No. 5   ,,   ,,
No. 2   ,,   ,, No. 7 ,,   ,,   No. 7   ,,   ,, No. 2   ,,   ,,

Every 6,000 miles (10000 km.) or 6 months

Distributor contact breaker gap

Remove the distributor cap and turn the crankshaft until the contacts are fully open. Check the gap (1) with a feeler gauge (see **'GENERAL DATA'**); the gauge should be a sliding fit in the gap. If the gap varies appreciably from the gauge thickness, slacken the contact plate securing screw (2) and adjust the contact gap by inserting a screwdriver in the notched hole at the end of the plate (3) and turning clockwise to decrease and anti-clockwise to increase the gap. Retighten the securing screw.

If the contact breaker points are burned or blackened, clean them with a fine carborundum stone or with fine emery-cloth, preferably after removing the lever carrying the moving contact, as described below.

Renewing points

'*A*'. One-piece '*Quikafit*' *type*. Remove the nut (4) and both the leads from the insulated post, then the securing screw (2) with its spring and plain washer, and lift off the complete contact set. If the removal of the moving contact alone is required, leave the screw (2) in position. When refitting, tighten the nut (4) until the leads are just pressing against the end of the spring, and give a further half turn only. Now set the contact breaker gap.

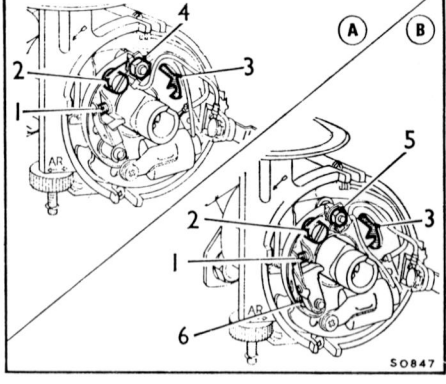

The distributor contact breaker

'A' One-piece 'Quikafit' type.
'B' Two-piece type.
1. Contact gap.
2. Securing screw.
3. Notched hole.
4. Nut—insulated post.
5. Nut—retaining post.
6. Large fibre washer.

'*B*'. *Two-piece type*. Unscrew the nut (5) securing the end of the spring, remove the plain washer and nylon insulator, both the leads, and lift off the contact lever assembly. Take out the screw (2) with its spring and plain washer and lift off the contact plate. When refitting, note that the large fibre washer (6) is fitted to the contact breaker pivot beneath the moving contact lever, the small fibre washer beneath the spring around the retaining post, and the lead terminals beneath the nylon insulator so that they make contact with the spring. Finally set the contact breaker gap.

NOTE.—A two-piece contact set cannot be fitted where 'Quikafit' contacts are original equipment.

48

Distributor advance mechanism

Check the functioning of the automatic advance and retard mechanism as follows:

Centrifugal: Remove the distributor cover and grasp the rotor arm (1) firmly. Turn the rotor in the direction of rotation and release it. The rotor arm should return to its original position without showing any tendency to stick.

Vacuum: Using a screwdriver, check that the plate (2) moves easily and smoothly to ensure that the vacuum-operated advance mechanism can operate.

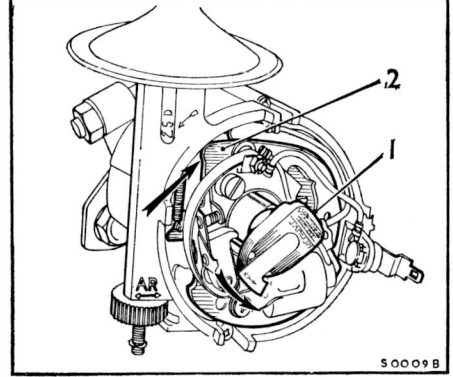

Check the distributor advance mechanism

1. Rotor.
2. Moving plate.

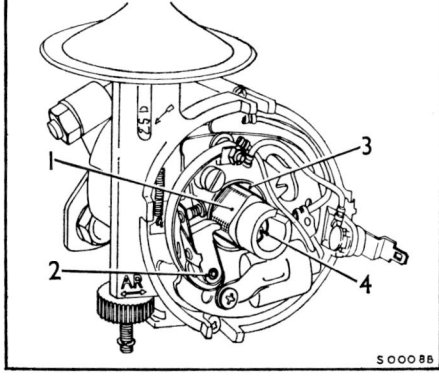

Distributor lubrication

1. Cam.
2. Contact breaker pivot.
3. Hole—centrifugal weights.
4. Cam spindle.

Distributor lubrication

Remove the distributor cover and rotor arm and lightly smear the cam (1) with grease or oil. **Avoid over-lubricating.**

Place a drop of oil or grease on the contact breaker pivot (2).

Add a few drops of oil to the following points:

Through the hole (3) in the contact breaker plate to lubricate the centrifugal weights. Around the screw (4) in the centre of the cam spindle (do not remove this screw as clearance is provided for oil to pass).

Carefully wipe away all surplus oil and see that the contact breaker points are perfectly clean and free of oil. Refit the rotor with its drive spindle engaging the spindle slot and push it on the shaft as far as it will go. Wipe the cover clean, and refit.

Every 6,000 miles (10000 km.) or 6 months

Battery specific gravity

Check the condition of the battery by taking hydrometer readings of the specific gravity of the electrolyte in each of the cells. Readings should not be taken immediately after topping up the cells. The specific gravity readings and their indications are as follows:

	For climates below 27° C. (80° F.)	For climates above 27° C. (80° F.)
Battery fully charged	1·270 to 1·290	1·210 to 1·230
Battery about half-discharged ..	1·190 to 1·210	1·130 to 1·150
Battery fully discharged	1·110 to 1·130	1·050 to 1·070

These figures are given assuming that the temperature of the solution is about 15° C. (60° F.). If the temperature of the electrolyte exceeds 15° C. (60° F.) ·002 must be added to the hydrometer reading for each 2·8° C. (5° F.) rise to give the true specific gravity. Similarly, ·002 must be subtracted from the hydrometer reading for every 2·8° C. (5° F.) below 15° C. (60° F.).

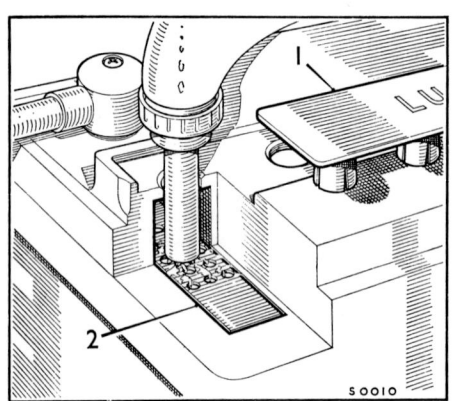

The Lucas D9 or DZ9 battery showing the manifold (1) and separator guard (2)

The readings for all cells should be approximately the same. If one cell gives a reading very different from the rest it may be that acid has spilled or has leaked from this particular cell, or there may be a short circuit between the plates, in which case the battery should be examined by a Distributor or Dealer.

Never leave the battery in a discharged condition for any length of time. Have it fully charged, and every fortnight give it a short refreshing charge to prevent any tendency for the plates to become permanently sulphated.

Sparking plugs

The sparking plugs should be cleaned every 6,000 miles (10000 km.), preferably with an air-blast service unit, and the gaps reset to the dimensions given in 'GENERAL DATA' on page 4.

Use a special Champion sparking plug gauge and setting tool, and move the side wire on the plug only, never the centre one.

Oily, dirty, or corroded plugs cannot give good results.

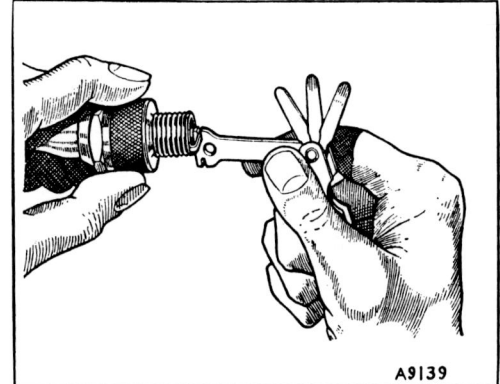

A Champion sparking plug gauge and setting tool

The lubricating hole for the dynamo end bearing

Dynamo bearing

Every 6,000 miles (10000 km.) add two or three drops of engine oil to the dynamo bearing through the central hole in the rear end bearing plate.

Do not over-oil.

Every 6,000 miles (10000 km.) or 6 months

Gearbox

Examine the oil level every 6,000 miles (10000 km.), and top up if necessary with one of the recommended engine oils.

The filler plug, which also serves to indicate the oil level, is located on the left-hand side of the gearbox beneath a rubber cover situated forward of the gear lever and is accessible when the rubber cover has been raised.

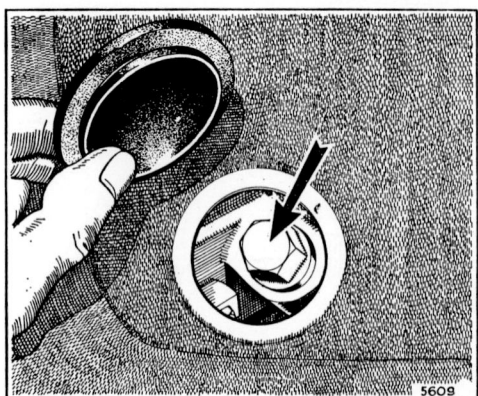

The gearbox filler and level plug. Clean round the plug thoroughly before removing

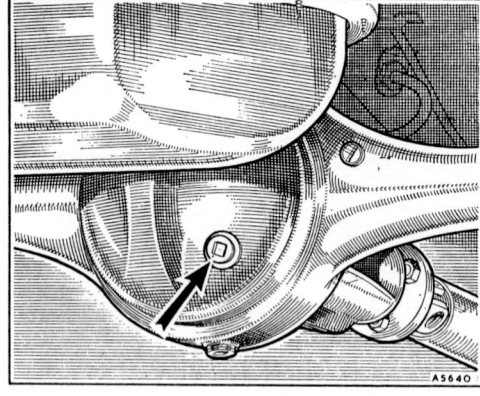

The rear axle combined filler and level plug

Rear axle

The oil level should be checked at intervals of 6,000 miles (10000 km.), and replenished if necessary.

The combined filler and level plug is located on the back of the axle casing and is accessible from underneath the car.

Insert a length of $\frac{7}{16}$ in. (11 mm.) square bar and use an open-ended spanner to remove the plug.

NOTE.—It is essential that only Hypoid oil be used in the rear axle.

Tracking the wheels

Excessive and uneven tyre wear is usually caused by faulty wheel tracking. The wheels should toe-in $\frac{3}{32}$ in. (2·4 mm.) to each other, but care must be exercised to ensure that the measurements are taken at axle level and that the rims run true. Correct setting of the front wheels entails the use of a wheel alignment gauge, and the owner is advised to **entrust the work to an authorized Distributor or Dealer.**

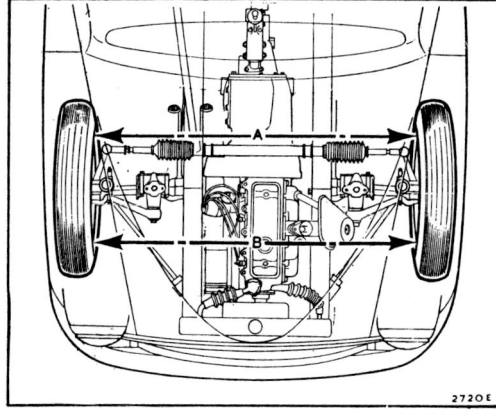

Front wheel alignment in the straight-ahead position. Dimension (A) must be $\frac{3}{32}$ in. (2·4 mm.) greater than dimension (B)

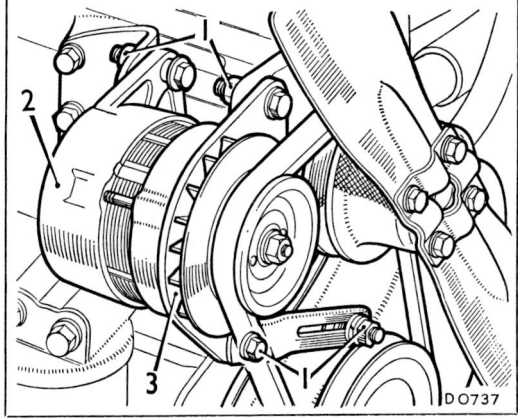

The alternator attachment bolts

1. Attachment bolts.
2. Slip-ring end cover.
3. Drive end bracket.

Alternator

Belt tension and adjustment

When correctly tensioned a deflection of $\frac{3}{8}$ to $\frac{1}{2}$ in. (10 to 13 mm.) under moderate hand pressure should be possible at a point midway on the longest belt run. To adjust, slacken the adjusting link and mounting bolts and lift or lever the alternator to tension the belt. Apply any leverage necessary to the drive end bracket only and not to any other part of the alternator. Use a lever preferably of wood or soft metal to avoid damaging the end bracket. Tighten the bolts and recheck the belt tension. DO NOT OVERTENSION as this will impose an excess loading on the drive bearings and stretch the belt unduly.

Cleaning

Clean the slip-ring end cover ventilating apertures.

For a complete summary of the 6,000 miles (10000 km.) or 6 months service refer to page 58.

Every 12,000 miles (20000 km.) or 12 months

Water pump

Every 12,000 miles (20000 km.) remove the plug (if fitted) from the water pump body and add a small quantity of grease.

The greasing of the water pump must be done very sparingly, otherwise grease will run past the bearings onto the face of the carbon sealing ring and impair its efficiency.

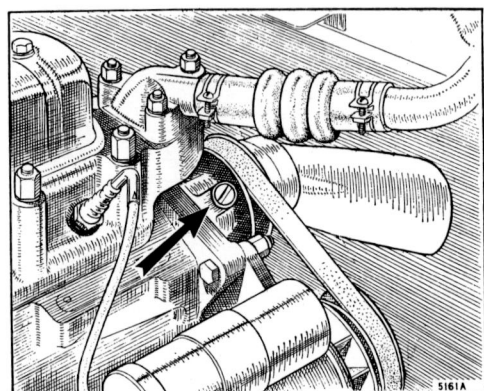

Unscrew the plug (if fitted) from the water pump body and lubricate the pump sparingly

The component parts of the air cleaner

1. Wing nut.
2. Element.
3. Body.
4. Casting and tie-rod.
5. Base and venturi.

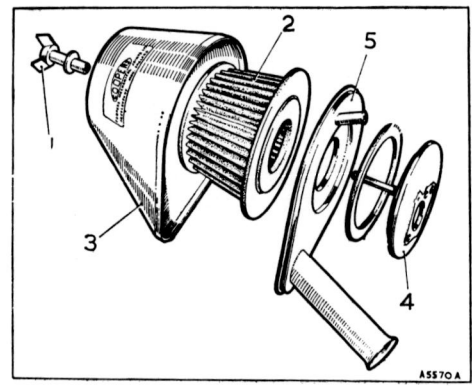

Air cleaner

The air cleaner element must be renewed every 12,000 miles (20000 km.), or earlier in dusty operating conditions. Unscrew the wing nut on the top of the air cleaner, lift off the body, and extract the element. Clean the body thoroughly before fitting the new element. Do not remove the body or disturb the element at any other time.

To obviate the possibility of the carburetter icing up when the vehicle is operated under cold conditions the air intake should be positioned adjacent to the exhaust manifold. During warmer weather it is advisable to move the intake away from the manifold.

Every 12,000 miles (20000 km.) or 12 months

Sparking plugs

Every 12,000 miles (20000 km.) a new set of sparking plugs of the recommended Champion type should be fitted (see page 4). To save fuel and to ensure easy starting the plugs should be cleaned and tested every 6,000 miles (10000 km.), or more often if conditions demand.

Steering rack and pinion

A lubrication point is provided on the rack housing and is accessible when the carpet above the gearbox cover has been turned back and the rubber plug removed. This nipple should be used to replenish the rack assembly with oil every 12,000 miles (20000 km.). Avoid overfilling the steering rack. Give no more than 10 strokes.

The steering rack lubricating nipple accessible through a hole in the floor

Steering and suspension

Every 12,000 miles (20000 km.) the steering and suspension moving parts should be thoroughly checked for wear. Any worn or damaged components should be renewed and adjustments carried out where necessary.

The rear spring 'U' bolts should be examined, and tightened if necessary.

Since the springs are rubber-mounted, oil or grease must not be applied to them.

ENGINE BREATHING
Filler cap

An air filter is incorporated in the oil filler cap (1), and is renewable as a complete assembly.

Every 12,000 miles (20000 km.) or 12 months

Control valve (10ME engine only)
Servicing
Remove the spring clip (2) and dismantle the valve. Clean all metal parts with a solvent (trichlorethylene, fuel, etc.). If deposits are difficult to remove, immerse in boiling water before applying the solvent. **DO NOT USE AN ABRASIVE.**

Clean the diaphragm (3) with detergent or methylated spirit. Replace components showing signs of wear or damage.

Reassemble the valve, making sure the metering needle (4) is in the cruciform guides (5) and the diaphragm is seated correctly.

Testing
Run the engine at idling speed and normal operating temperature and remove the oil filler cap. If the valve is functioning correctly the engine speed will increase by approximately 200 r.p.m.; this change can be detected by ear. If there is no change in engine speed the valve must be renewed.

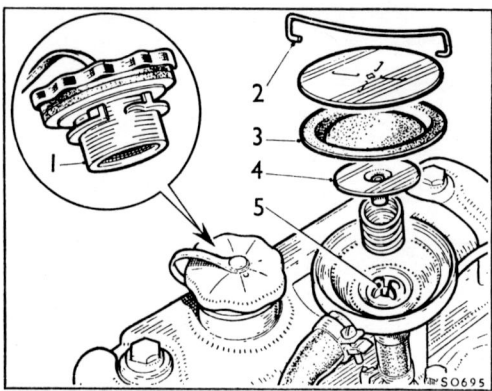

The breather control valve components

1. Combined air filter/oil filler cap.
10ME engine only.
2. Spring clip.
3. Diaphragm.
4. Metering needle.
5. Cruciform guides.

For a complete summary of the 12,000 miles (20000 km.) or 12 months service refer to page 59.

AS INDICATED BY THE WARNING LIGHT (when fitted)

Oil filter warning light
The oil filter warning light, which is incorporated in the instrument dial, is a guide to the need for a more frequent oil and filter element change. If the light comes on and continues to glow when the engine is running at or above fast idling speed, it indicates the need for a new oil filter element and an oil change: this should be done as soon as possible within a maximum of a further 300 miles (500 km.).

If 6,000 miles or six months have passed since the last oil and filter change, although the warning light has not appeared, both the engine oil and filter element must be changed.

MAINTENANCE SUMMARY

Weekly

Inspect engine oil level, and top up as necessary.

See that the radiator is full to within $\frac{1}{2}$ in. (13 mm.) of the bottom of the filler neck.

Check battery, and top up if necessary.

Check tyre pressures.

Check road wheel nuts for tightness (do not overtighten).

3,000 miles (5000 km.) or 3 months service

1. *Engine*
   Top up carburetter piston damper.
   Top up radiator.
   Top up windscreen washer bottle.

2. *Clutch*
   Check clutch pedal free movement, and adjust if necessary.
   Lubricate clutch pedal shaft and linkage.

3. *Brakes*
   Check brakes, and adjust if necessary.
   Make visual inspection of brake lines and pipes.
   Check level of fluid in the master cylinder, and top up if necessary.
   Lubricate brake pedal shaft and linkage.

4. *Electrical*
   Check battery, and top up to correct level.
   Check headlamp alignment.

5. *Lubrication*
   Lubricate all grease nipples (except steering rack and pinion).
   Top up engine oil level.

6. *Wheels and tyres*
   Check tyre pressures, including spare.

NOTE.—Take the advice of your Distributor or Dealer on the need for:
   (a) More frequent oil changes;
   (b) Changing round road wheels.

MAINTENANCE SUMMARY

6,000 miles (10000 km.) or 6 months service

1. *Engine*
   Top up carburetter piston damper.
   Top up radiator.
   Check fan belt tension.
   Check valve rocker clearances, and adjust if necessary.
   Top up windscreen washer bottle.

2. *Ignition*
   Check functioning of automatic advance and retard mechanism.
   Lubricate all distributor parts as necessary.
   Check and adjust distributor contact points.
   Clean and adjust sparking plugs.

3. *Clutch*
   Check clutch pedal free movement, and adjust if necessary.
   Lubricate clutch pedal shaft and linkage.

4. *Steering*
   Check front wheel alignment, and adjust if necessary.

5. *Brakes*
   Check brakes, and adjust if necessary.
   Make visual inspection of brake lines and pipes.
   Check level of fluid in the master cylinder, and top up if necessary.
   Lubricate brake pedal shaft linkage.

6. *Electrical*
   Check battery cell specific gravity readings, and top up to correct level.
   Lubricate dynamo bearing.
   Check all lamps for correct functioning.
   Check headlamp alignment.

7. *Lubrication*
   Change oil in engine.
   Fit new oil filter element.
   Top up gearbox and rear axle oil levels.
   Lubricate all grease nipples (except steering rack and pinion).
   Lubricate door locks and hinges.

8. *Wheels and tyres*
   Check tyre pressures, including spare.

9,000 miles (15000 km.) or 9 months service
   Carry out the **3,000 miles (5000 km.) or 3 months service.**

MAINTENANCE SUMMARY

12,000 miles (20000 km.) or 12 months service

1. *Engine*
   Check valve rocker clearances, and adjust if necessary.
   Top up carburetter piston damper.
   Top up radiator.
   Check fan belt tension.
   Lubricate water pump sparingly with grease (if plug fitted).
   Fit new oil filler cap and filter assembly.
   Test and clean breather control valve (10ME engine).
   Fit new air cleaner element.
   Top up windscreen washer bottle.

2. *Ignition*
   Check functioning of automatic advance and retard mechanism.
   Lubricate all distributor parts as necessary.
   Check and adjust distributor points.
   Fit new sparking plugs.

3. *Clutch*
   Check clutch pedal free movement, and adjust if necessary.
   Lubricate clutch pedal shaft and linkage.

4. *Steering*
   Check steering and suspension moving parts for wear.
   Check front wheel alignment, and adjust if necessary.

5. *Brakes*
   Check brakes, and adjust if necessary.
   Inspect and clean out brake linings and drums.
   Make visual inspection of brake lines and pipes.
   Check level of fluid in the master cylinder, and top up if necessary.
   Lubricate brake pedal shaft and linkage.

6. *General*
   Check rear road spring seat bolts for tightness.

7. *Electrical*
   Check battery cell specific gravity readings and top up to correct level.
   Lubricate dynamo bearing.
   Check all lamps for correct functioning.
   Check headlamp alignment.

8. *Lubrication*
   Change engine oil.
   Fit new oil filter element.
   Top up gearbox and rear axle.
   Lubricate all grease nipples.
   Lubricate steering rack and pinion.
   Lubricate door locks and hinges.

9. *Wheels and tyres*
   Check tyre pressures, including spare.

THE SERVICE EXCHANGE SCHEME

The Service Exchange Scheme has been designed as a money-saver.

The scheme covers a range of assemblies for vehicles produced in the last 10 years. Your Distributor or Dealer will supply any exchange unit offered for your vehicle at a price which allows for the return of the old one to us for rebuilding to 'as new' standard, at one of our specialist factories or by the original supplier.

The use of this technique reduces the cost but not the quality, and each replacement unit carries the same warranty as a brand new one.

Ask your Distributor or Dealer for full details and for examples of the money you can save by taking advantage of the scheme.

IDENTIFICATION

When communicating with your Distributor or Dealer always quote the car and engine numbers. When the communication concerns the transmission units or body details it is necessary to quote also the transmission casing and body numbers.

Car number. This is stamped on the identification plate which is secured to the right-hand side of the dash panel beneath the bonnet and should be quoted complete with all prefixes.

Engine number. Every engine carries a serial number stamped on the block or a metal plate which is secured to the right-hand side of the cylinder block.

The letter 'H' or 'L' preceding the engine number denotes either a High or Low compression engine.

Gearbox number. This is stamped on the gearbox casing forward of the change speed lever turret.

Rear axle number. This is stamped on the front of the left-hand axle tube adjacent to the spring seat.

Body number. This is stamped on a plate welded to the left-hand tie-plate between the radiator and wing valance.

Ignition key number. To reduce the possibility of theft, ignition switches on later cars are **not** marked with a number. Owners are advised to make a note of the number stamped on their ignition key in case of future loss.

HYDRAULIC BRAKE SYSTEMS

In addition to the recommended periodical inspection of brake components it is advisable as the car ages and as a precaution against the effects of wear and deterioration, to make a more searching inspection and renew parts as necessary.

It is recommended that:

1. Disc brake pads, drum brake linings, hoses and pipes should be examined at intervals no greater than those laid down in the Passport to Service.
2. Brake fluid should be changed completely every 18 months or 24,000 miles (40000 km.) whichever is the sooner.
3. All fluid seals in the hydraulic system and all flexible hoses should be examined and renewed if necessary every 3 years or 40,000 miles (65000 km.) whichever is the sooner. At the same time the working surface of the pistons and of the bores of the master cylinder, wheel cylinders and other slave cylinders should be examined and new parts fitted where necessary.

Care must always be taken to observe the following points:

(a) At all times use the recommended fluid.
(b) Never leave fluid in unsealed containers. It absorbs moisture quickly and can be dangerous if used in your braking system in this condition.
(c) Fluid drained from the system or used for bleeding is best discarded.
(d) The necessity for absolute cleanliness throughout cannot be over-emphasized.

SUPPLEMENTARY TOOL KIT

To supplement the tool kit a waterproof canvas roll containing the following is obtainable from all Distributors. Part No. AKF 1596 should be quoted.

6 spanners: $\frac{5}{16}$ in. $\times \frac{3}{8}$ in. A.F.
$\frac{7}{16}$ in. $\times \frac{1}{2}$ in. A.F.
$\frac{1}{2}$ in. $\times \frac{9}{16}$ in. A.F.
$\frac{9}{16}$ in. $\times \frac{5}{8}$ in. A.F.
$\frac{11}{16}$ in. $\times \frac{13}{16}$ in. A.F.
$\frac{3}{4}$ in. $\times \frac{7}{8}$ in. A.F.

1 pair 6 in. pliers.
1 tommy-bar (7 in. $\times \frac{3}{8}$ in. diameter).
1 tubular spanner ($\frac{1}{2}$ in. $\times \frac{9}{16}$ in. A.F.).
2 screwdrivers.

LUBRICATION DIAGRAM

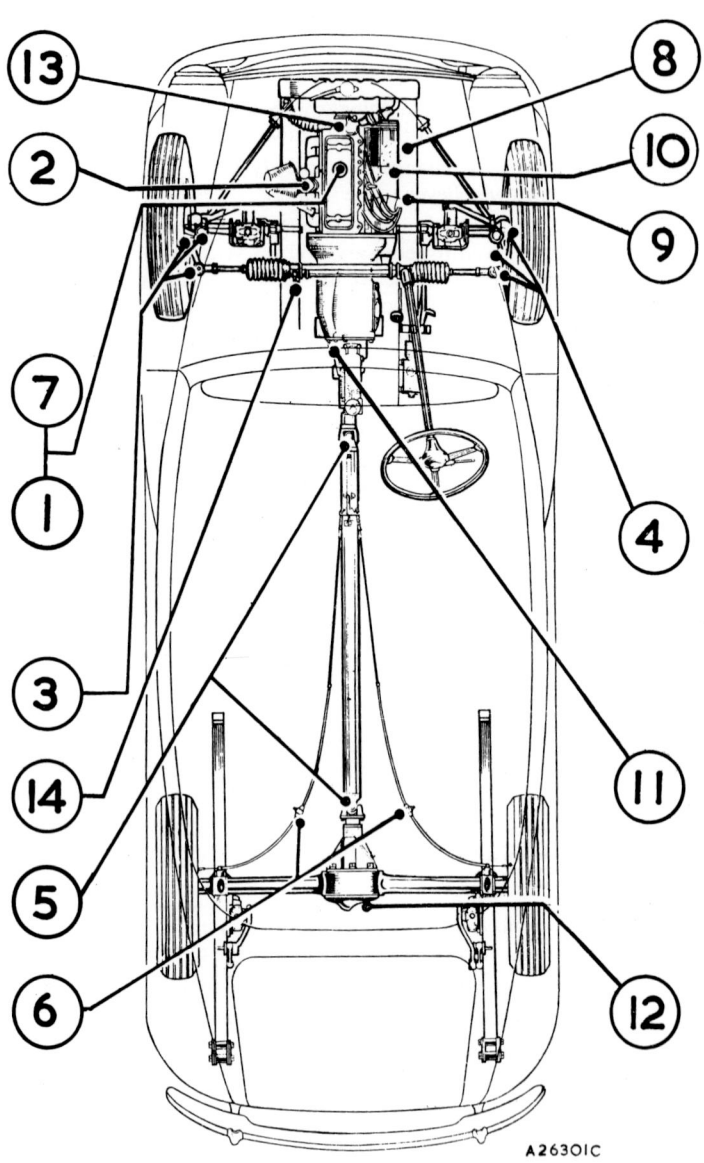

A26301C

KEY TO DIAGRAM

Ensure that the vehicle is standing on a level surface when checking oil levels.

Weekly

(1)   ENGINE. Inspect the oil level with the dipstick, and replenish if necessary.

Every 3,000 miles (5000 km.) or 3 months

(2)   CARBURETTER. Remove the damper unit and pour oil into the hollow piston rod to a point $\frac{1}{2}$ in. (13 mm.) above the top of the rod. Under no circumstances should a heavy lubricant be used.

(3) and (4). STEERING JOINT NIPPLES. Give three or four strokes of a gun filled with grease.

(5)   PROPELLER SHAFT NIPPLES. Give three or four strokes of a gun filled with grease.

(6)   HAND BRAKE CABLE NIPPLES. Give three or four strokes of a gun filled with grease.

Every 6,000 miles (10000 km.) or 6 months

(7)   ENGINE. Drain off the old oil and refill with new oil.

(8)   OIL FILTER. Wash the bowl in fuel and fit a new element.

(9)   DISTRIBUTOR. Withdraw the rotor arm and add a few drops of oil to the cam bearing and to the advance mechanism through the gap around the cam spindle. Smear the distributor cam spindle and contact breaker pivot with grease.

(10)   DYNAMO. Add a few drops of oil through the hole in the commutator end bearing.

(11)   GEARBOX. Inspect the oil level, and replenish if necessary with oil.

(12)   REAR AXLE. Remove the filler plug, and replenish if necessary to the filler plug level with hypoid gear oil.

Every 12,000 miles (20000 km.) or 12 months

(13)   WATER PUMP. Remove the plug (if fitted) from the water pump body and lubricate the pump sparingly with grease.

(14)   STEERING RACK. Apply an oil gun to the nipple on the steering rack and give up to 10 strokes using hypoid gear oil.

Recommended oils and greases are given on page 66.

INDEX

Page

A

Air cleaner 54

B

Body
Bonnet 7, 14
Bright trim 12
Coachwork 12
Door locks 13
Hood (Convertible) .. 15–16
Interior 12
Luggage compartment .. 15
Roof rack 16
Seat adjustment 7
Seat belts 17
Seat, folding (Traveller) .. 14
Windscreen 12
Woodwork, exterior (Traveller) 12
Brakes
Adjustment 42
Fluid 41
Hand brake 6, 43
Master cylinder 41
Systems (hydraulic) 61
Bulbs, replacement 38

C

Carburetter
Adjustment 40
Induction heaters 20
Piston 41
Car number 60
Clutch adjustment 44
Controls
Choke (mixture) 7
Gear lever 6
Hand brake 6
Heater 10–11
Pedals 6
Windscreen washer 9
Cooling system
Draining 24
Fan belt 46
Frost precautions 25
Radiator filling .. 20, 24

D

Data, general 4, 5

Page

E

Electrical equipment
Alternator 38, 53
Battery 45, 50
Direction indicators .. 7, 29–31
Fuses 26
Headlamps 27–29
Number-plate lamp 31
Panel light 31
Roof lamp 38
Sidelamps 29–30
Stop/tail lamps .. 30–31
Voltage regulators 26
Warning lights .. 7–9, 31
Wiring diagrams .. 32–37
Engine number 60

F

Foreword 3
Fuel system
Filling up 20
Fuel gauge 9

I

Ignition
Distributor 48, 49
Sparking plugs .. 51, 55
Timing 39

J

Jacking 22–23

L

Lubrication
Carburetter damper 41
Diagram 62, 63
Distributor 49
Dynamo 51
Engine.. .. .. 19, 46–47
Gearbox 52
Grease points.. .. 43, 44
Oil filter 47
Rear axle 52
Recommended lubricants .. 66
Steering rack and pinion .. 55
Warning lights 9, 56
Water pump 54

Page

M

Maintenance attention
    Every 3,000 miles ..   41–45
    Every 6,000 miles ..   46–53
    Every 12,000 miles ..   54–55
    Summary   57–59

R

Reclining front seats 16

S

Seat belts   17–18
Service Exchange Scheme .. 60
Starting up 20
Supplementary tool kit .. 60
Switches
    Dipper 7
    Direction indicator 7
    Horn 7
    Ignition and starter 8
    Lighting 9
    Panel light 9
    Roof lamp 9
    Windscreen wiper 9

Page

T

Tyres
    Care of   21–23
    Fitting 23
    Interchanging.. 22
    Pressures 4
    Size 4

V

Valve rocker clearance .. 47

W

Wheels
    Alignment 52
    Removing 23
    Spare 22
Windscreen wiper 27
Wiring diagrams .. 32–37

RECOMMENDED LUBRICANTS

Component	Engine, Gearbox, and Carburetter			Steering Rack and Rear Axle		Grease Points	Upper Cylinder Lubrication
	All temperatures above −10° C. (10° F.)	Temperatures −15° to −5° C. (0° to 20° F.)	All temperatures below −15° C. (0° F.)	All temperatures above −10° C. (10° F.)	All temperatures below −5° C. (20° F.)		
Climatic conditions						All conditions	All conditions
Viscosity requirement	S.A.E. 10W/50 S.A.E. 10W/40 S.A.E. 20/50 or S.A.E. 20W/40	S.A.E. 10W/50 S.A.E. 10W/40 or S.A.E. 10W/30	S.A.E. 5W/30 or S.A.E. 5W/20	S.A.E. 90 Hypoid	S.A.E. 80 Hypoid		
Minimum performance level	MIL–L–2104B	MIL–L–2104B	MIL–L–2104B	MIL–L–2105B	MIL–L–2105B		
MOBIL	Mobiloil Special 20W/50 or Super 10W/50	Mobiloil Super 10W/50	Mobiloil 5W/20	Mobilube G.X. 90	Mobilube G.X. 80	Mobilgrease M.P.	Mobil Upperlube
BP	BP Super Visco-Static 20W–50	BP Super Visco-Static 10W–50	BP Super Visco-Static 5W–20	BP Gear Oil S.A.E. 90 E.P.	BP Gear Oil S.A.E. 80 E.P.	BP Energrease L. 2	BP Upper Cylinder Lubricant
SHELL	Shell Super Motor Oil 100 (20W/50)	Shell Super Motor Oil 101 (10W/30)	Shell Winter Special Motor Oil or Shell Super Motor Oil 5W/30	Spirax 90 E.P.	Spirax 80 E.P.	Shell Retinax A	Shell Upper Cylinder Lubricant
FILTRATE	Filtrate Super 20W/50	Filtrate Super 10W/30	Filtrate 5W/20	Filtrate E.P. Gear 90	Filtrate E.P. Gear 80	Filtrate Super Lithium Grease	Filtrate Petroyle
STERNOL	Sternol Super W.W. Motor Oil	Sternol Super W.W. Multigrade 10W/40	Sternol W.W. Multigrade 5W/20	Sternol Ambroleum E.P. 90 or E.P. 90/140	Sternol Ambroleum E.P. 80	Sternol Ambroline Grease LHT 2	Sternol Magikoyl
DUCKHAMS	Duckhams Q. 20–50	Duckhams Q. 5500	Duckhams Q. 5–30	Duckhams Hypoid 90	Duckhams Hypoid 80	Duckhams L.B. 10 Grease	Duckhams Adcoid Liquid
CASTROL	Castrol GTX or Castrol XL 20W/50	Castrolite or Castrol Super	Castrol CRI 5W/20	Castrol Hypoy	Castrol Hypoy Light	Castrol L.M. Grease	Castrollo
ESSO	Esso Extra Motor Oil 20W/50 or Esso Uniflow	Esso Extra Motor Oil 10W/40 or Esso Uniflow	Esso Extra Motor Oil 5W/20	Esso Gear Oil G 90/140 or G.P. 90	Esso Gear Oil G.P. 80	Esso Multipurpose Grease H	Esso Upper Cylinder Lubricant

ADDENDUM

Ignition/starter switch and steering lock (when fitted)

Unlock

To unlock the steering, insert the key and turn it to the 'I' position. If the steering-wheel has been turned to engage the lock, slight movement of the steering-wheel will assist disengagement of the lock plunger. The key must be in the 'I' position when towing the vehicle for recovery.

Ignition and start

To switch on the ignition turn the key to the 'II' position. Further movement against spring resistance to the 'III' position operates the starter motor. Release the key immediately the engine starts.

Lock

To lock the steering, turn the key anti-clockwise to the position marked 'I', press the key inwards and turn the key to the 'O' position and withdraw it. The lock will engage when the steering-wheel is turned.

Key numbers

To reduce the possibility of theft, locks are not marked with a number. It is important that owners **MAKE A NOTE OF THE KEY NUMBERS IMMEDIATELY** on taking delivery of the car and at the same time consult their Distributor or Dealer regarding steering lock key replacements.

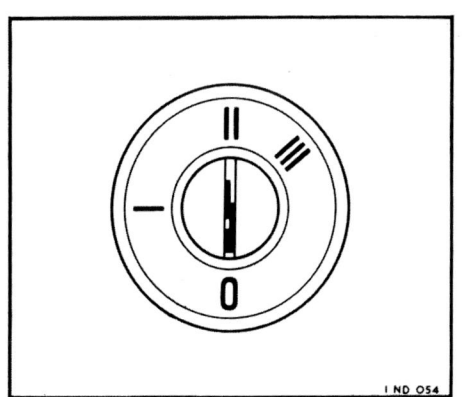

I NO 054

WARNING. — The steering lock ignition starter switch and its electrical circuits are designed to prevent the ignition system and starter from being energized while the steering lock is engaged. **Serious consequences could result from alterations to or substitution of the steering lock/ignition switch or its wiring. In no circumstances must the ignition switch be separated from the steering lock.**

Printed and distributed by Brooklands Books Ltd., PO Box 146, Cobham,
Surrey KT11 1LG, England Phone: 01932 865051 Fax: 01932 868803
E-mail: sales@brooklands-books.com

MORRIS MINOR SERIES MM, Series II and 1000 Official Workshop Manual

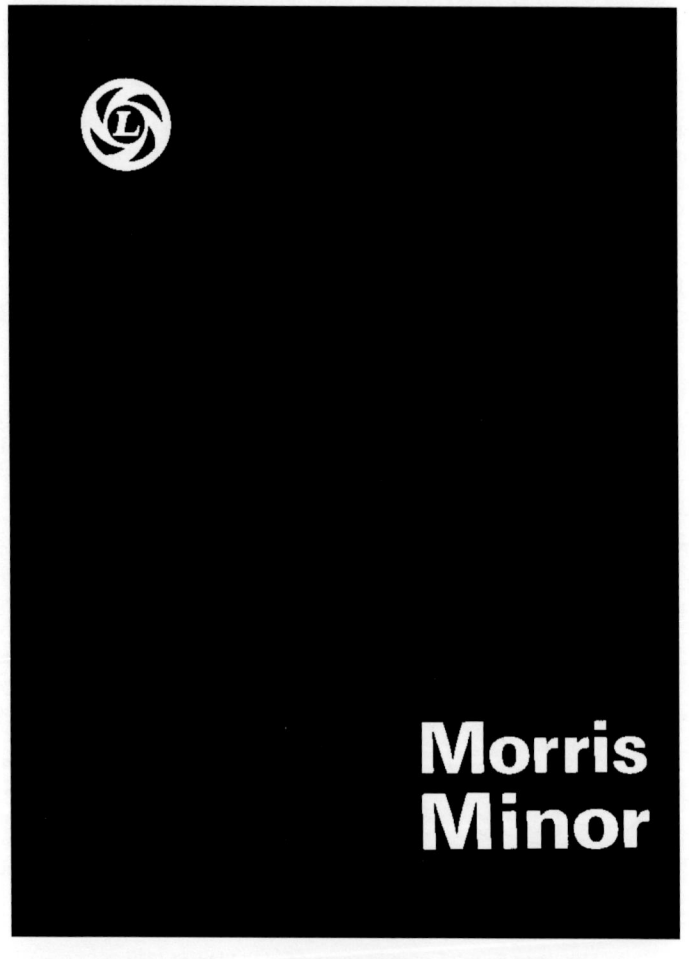

Morris Minor

AKD530   **440 pages**   **Soft Bound**

Available from Morris Minor specialists or
in case of difficulty from:
Brooklands Books Ltd. PO Box 146,
Cobham, Surrey KT11 1LG, England
Phone: 01932 865051 Fax: 01932 868803

www.brooklands-books.com